WONDERS OF EARTH

Visit us at **www.kidsbooks.com**

Contents

Introduction 6

Our Watery Planet 7
by Celia Bland

In Nature's Path 32
by Stella Sands

Science Old and New 56
by Rebecca L. Grambo

Earth's Treasures 82
by Donald Olson

Glossary 106

Index 107

INTRODUCTION

Have you ever stopped to think about the amazing planet on which we live? On your way to school, do you stop to think about the ground you walk on, or the sky above you? It is easy to take our natural world for granted.

Wonders of Earth will open up the treasure chest that is our planet. From the depths of the ocean to the peaks of the highest mountain, this book will introduce you to creatures and phenomena that you never knew about. You will learn about what lies at the bottom of the ocean, what the planet is made of, how creatures—including humans—make the most of what Earth provides, and how nature can shake things up with a violent storm or earth-shattering quake.

In the pages that follow you can explore the world around you and get lost in the wonders of Earth. Let the journey begin!

OUR WATERY PLANET

Like the landscape of an alien planet in a science-fiction movie, the world under the sea is filled with bizarre creatures and breathtaking beauty. From fish that live so deep in the ocean that they have to create their own source of light, to colorful coral reefs that stretch for hundreds of miles, the sea is filled with astounding splendors just waiting to be discovered!

WATERY PLANET

If you were to rocket into space and look back at Earth, you would see a big blue planet. It looks blue because most of Earth's surface is covered with water. The sea, in fact, has one thousand times more room for living creatures than air and land combined.

GREAT OCEANS

The Pacific, Atlantic, Indian, and Arctic oceans cover over two-thirds of our planet. That's more than 300 million square miles! The Pacific is by far the deepest and the largest ocean. It covers more than one-third of the globe.

PASS THE SALT

What's the saltiest ocean? The Atlantic. Rocks make the water salty. Waves erode the rocks, which contain salt that dissolves in the water. Some sea animals can't live in very salty waters. Others, like clams and oysters, use the calcium found in sea salt to build their shells.

Salt literally drips from rocks near the Red Sea—one of the saltiest seas on the planet.

WATER RE-CYCLE

How do Earth's oceans remain so full of water? The answer is in the water cycle. When water evaporates from the sea it becomes rain clouds. When the rain falls onto land, it drains into rivers. Then the rivers take water back to the sea.

DOWN UNDER

Home to many fascinating creatures, and burial ground for countless shipwrecks, the sea is a gold mine to adventurous types. Divers investigate animal behavior, recover ancient wrecks, and discover new marine species.

A diver observes a giant seajelly in action. ▼

FIRE AND ICE

Close to the equator, where the climate is hotter than anywhere else on Earth, sea water is warm. Farthest from the equator lies the Arctic Ocean, home of glaciers, icebergs, and animals specially adapted to wintry weather. Here the sea is icy cold.

SEA STUDY

Scientists who study the oceans are called *marine biologists*. They try to figure out how and why the oceans change, and why certain sea creatures and plants live in one place and not in another.

NOW AND THEN

About 6,000 years ago the ancient Egyptians invented sails. Over the centuries, sailing became a vital means of transportation and industry. Today, sailing is a pastime and a sport. One of the world's most famous ocean sailing races is the America's Cup.

WHO LIVES HERE?

Try to imagine all the living things in the world—more than 10 million species of animals, plants, fungi, bacteria, and other types of creatures! Does it come as a surprise that only 20 percent live on land? The remaining 80 percent are found in the sea.

◀ The octopus was once thought to be a monster.

▲ The hermit crab scuttles across the sea floor.

SINK OR SWIM

When you think of water, you probably think of swimming. But not all sea creatures spend their life swishing their fins like fishes or whales do. Many plants and animals live on the sea floor. Tiny plants and animals known as plankton simply float on the ocean currents.

◀ The wide-mouthed manta ray easily gobbles up some plankton.

UP FOR AIR

Sea mammals, such as whales and dolphins, cannot spend all of their time under the water's surface like fish. They must come up to breathe, as people must do when in the water. However, sea mammals can dive for long periods of time. The sperm whale can stay underwater for more than an hour, holding its breath while hunting giant squid.

HOMEBODIES

Many sea creatures stay in one area of an ocean their whole life. Certain animals, such as the giant whale shark at right, roam the waters for food.

Hatched in rivers, salmon live in the ocean during their adult life. But when it comes time to spawn, or produce young, salmon leave the ocean and swim back to the river where they were born.

STAYING ALIVE

As a lower link on the food chain, small fish have developed a great defense—swimming in schools. Because the fish swim together, darting left and right, predators have a hard time picking out a single fish to catch.

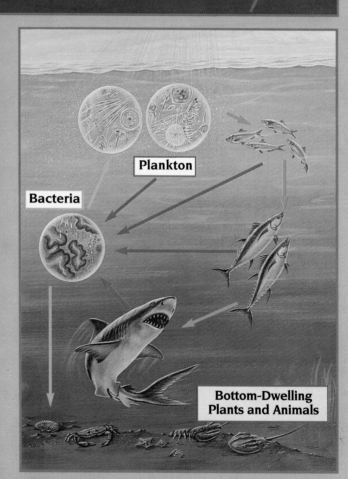

Plankton

Bacteria

Bottom-Dwelling Plants and Animals

THE FOOD CHAIN

Like any chain, a food chain is made of links—living creatures eating other living things. It all starts with bacteria, which is partly dependent on the decomposition of dead animals. Bacteria provides nutrients to plankton and other sea life. Then plankton are eaten by small animals who are in turn eaten by larger animals.

11

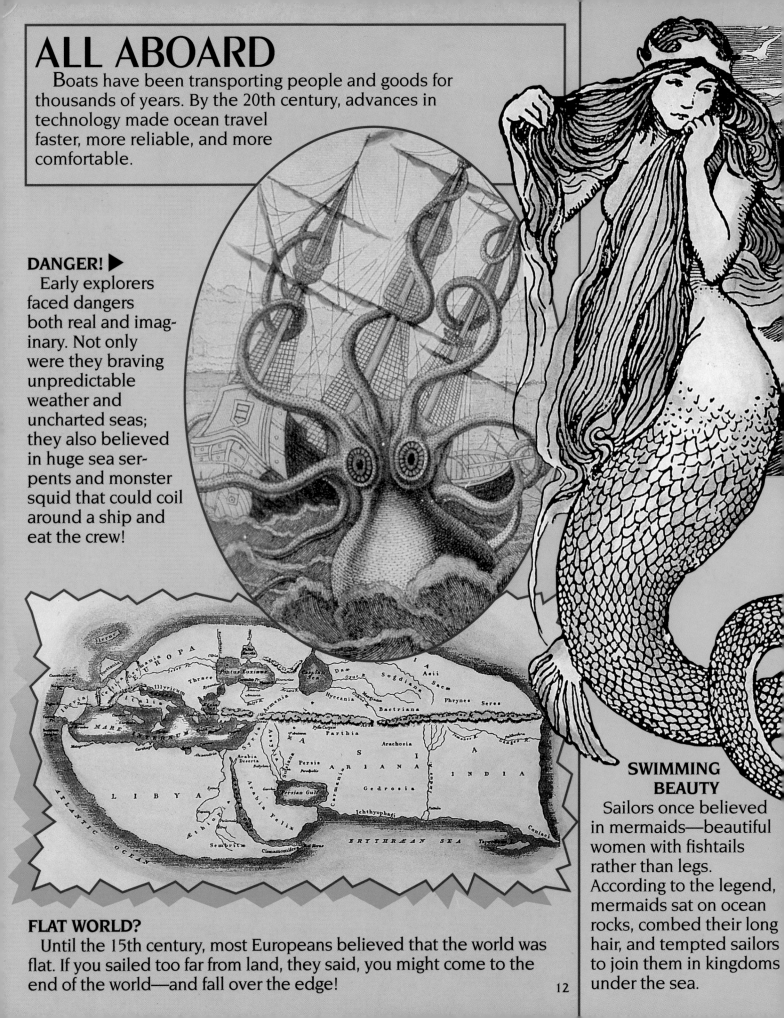

ALL ABOARD

Boats have been transporting people and goods for thousands of years. By the 20th century, advances in technology made ocean travel faster, more reliable, and more comfortable.

DANGER! ▶

Early explorers faced dangers both real and imaginary. Not only were they braving unpredictable weather and uncharted seas; they also believed in huge sea serpents and monster squid that could coil around a ship and eat the crew!

SWIMMING BEAUTY

Sailors once believed in mermaids—beautiful women with fishtails rather than legs. According to the legend, mermaids sat on ocean rocks, combed their long hair, and tempted sailors to join them in kingdoms under the sea.

FLAT WORLD?

Until the 15th century, most Europeans believed that the world was flat. If you sailed too far from land, they said, you might come to the end of the world—and fall over the edge!

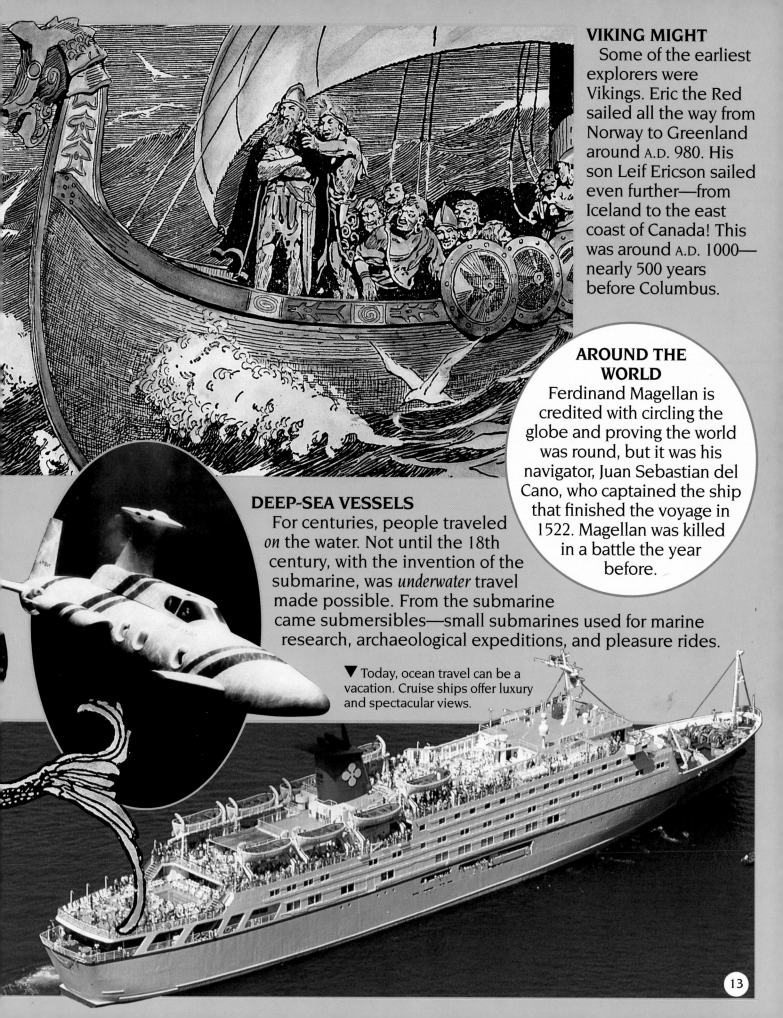

VIKING MIGHT

Some of the earliest explorers were Vikings. Eric the Red sailed all the way from Norway to Greenland around A.D. 980. His son Leif Ericson sailed even further—from Iceland to the east coast of Canada! This was around A.D. 1000—nearly 500 years before Columbus.

AROUND THE WORLD

Ferdinand Magellan is credited with circling the globe and proving the world was round, but it was his navigator, Juan Sebastian del Cano, who captained the ship that finished the voyage in 1522. Magellan was killed in a battle the year before.

DEEP-SEA VESSELS

For centuries, people traveled *on* the water. Not until the 18th century, with the invention of the submarine, was *underwater* travel made possible. From the submarine came submersibles—small submarines used for marine research, archaeological expeditions, and pleasure rides.

▼ Today, ocean travel can be a vacation. Cruise ships offer luxury and spectacular views.

13

ON THE MOVE

The ocean stays in motion. Even when the water seems calm—waves, tides, and currents keep the waters flowing.

CURRENT EVENTS

Not until the 20th century did people begin to understand the ocean's currents. In the Northern Hemisphere, currents sweep clockwise from the equator to the Arctic. In the Southern Hemisphere, they travel counterclockwise.

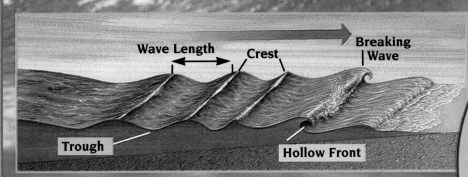

Wave Length　Crest　Breaking | Wave

Trough　Hollow Front

MAKING WAVES

How do waves form? Wind blowing along the sea's surface drags the top of the water and creates waves. As a wave moves closer to shore, the water below the wave gets shallow. This makes the wave taller until it moves into even shallower water, topples over, and breaks.

TIME AND TIDE

Tides are caused by the sun and moon's gravitational pulls. As Earth turns on its axis, the moon's gravity pulls the ocean toward it, creating high tide on the parts of Earth closest and farthest away from the moon. At the same time, the areas in between will experience low tide. Each part of the planet has two high tides and two low tides per day.

BIG BOARDS

Surfing has been an exciting sport since A.D. 400, when it was invented by the Polynesians in the Pacific. The first Westerner to witness surfing was Captain James Cook at Kealakekua Bay, Hawaii, in 1778. The surfboards, shaped from trees, were 20 feet long and weighed as much as 200 pounds!

◀ KILLER WAVES

Tidal waves, or *tsunamis*, don't actually have any connection to tides. They are caused by seismic activity on the sea floor. Tsunamis can travel hundreds of miles, growing sometimes hundreds of feet high, and reaching speeds of 500 mph.

WATER SPORTS ▼

A combination surfboard and sail, "sailboards" are speedy and acrobatic. Some windsurfers have been clocked at 50 mph, moving faster than any other sailing craft!

▲ KON-TIKI EXPEDITION

In 1947, explorer Thor Heyerdahl built a simple wooden ship similar to the one used by early peoples. He wanted to test whether Indians from South America could have sailed the seas to settle Polynesia. It took him 101 days to sail from Peru to Polynesia, which proved the early expedition possible.

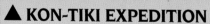

MEETING THE LAND

The coast can be a loud and dramatic place, where rocky cliffs are hit hard by breaking waves. Coastal creatures have to cling to rocks to keep from washing out to sea. Barnacles, snails, and bivalves (such as mussels and some types of scallops) attach themselves to coastal rocks with a sticky secretion produced in their bodies.

PUDDLE DWELLERS

When the tide goes out, puddles of water are left on shore. Seastars, seaweed, periwinkle snails, crabs, and sea urchins make their homes in these tide pools.

SHELL TREASURES

Have you ever found a queen conch shell on the beach? How about a tiger cowry or a rosy harp? These beached shells were once the homes of soft-bodied animals known as shellfish, or mollusks. Empty shells are popular collectible items for beachcombers.

16

WEED FOREST

Kelp, or seaweed, grows in "forests," taking root on hard sea floors near shore. The fastest-growing plant, kelp can gain as much as three feet a day, and reach lengths of 213 feet! Kelp floats upward instead of sinking because its stems are surrounded by gas-filled bulbs.

OTTER HANG-OUT

Kelp forests serve many purposes for the sea otter. During the day, otters eat the abalone, crabs, and urchins that feed there. At night they wrap themselves in the kelp fronds, and the waves rock them to sleep.

CITY OF CORAL

One of the most colorful and populated areas of the sea is in and around a coral reef. The bright colors of the coral are caused by algae that live inside. Outside the coral, schools of tropical fishes dazzle the eye with an equally fascinating display of color.

NO TOUCHING!

One of the best ways to appreciate the living treasures of a coral reef is to see it up close. Snorkelers and scuba divers flock to reefs. But they are careful never to touch the coral because that can damage or kill it.

IT'S ALIVE!

Coral may look and feel stony, but it is not rock. It's the skeleton of a living animal called a polyp. The polyps grow a skeleton on the outside to protect and support their soft bodies. Because the reef-building corals cannot live in water colder than 64°F, they are found only in warmer waters.

FEEDING TIME

All animals have to eat, including coral polyps. How do they do it when they are attached to the ocean floor? Coral polyps have tiny arms that catch plankton and pass it into their mouths.

THREE REEFS

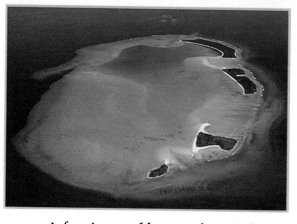

Reefs grow in different ways. A *fringing* reef is attached to the shore. An *atoll*, like the one shown at left, is a ring of coral formed around a sunken volcano. A *barrier* reef has a channel of water between it and the shore. Australia's Great Barrier Reef is a whopping 1,250 miles long. That makes it the biggest structure ever built by animals.

COAT OF ARMOR

You can often count on finding clownfish with the grasslike sea anemone. Unlike most sea life, the clownfish is safe from the anemone's stinging cells because of a thick, slimy mucous on its body.

Brain coral

KNOW YOUR CORAL

Stony corals, or hard corals, such as brain corals, form reefs. Gorgonians, or soft corals, such as sea fans, grow on the sea floor and on reefs, and look a lot like ferns or bushes.

CORAL POPULATION

Every coral reef has a population consisting of thousands of different animals that live and thrive there—including shellfish, moray eels, sea horses, and sharks.

SEASCAPES

Under the ocean, there is a landscape as varied as the one above water—with gigantic canyons, vast plains, tall mountains, and deep caves.

AGE-OLD SEA

When plants and animals die in the ocean, their remains drift down to the sea bottom. Drilling deep with special tools, scientists take samples of this sediment. The samples provide a rich history of millions of years of ocean life.

At the center of the Atlantic Ocean is a mountainous ridge surrounded by plains and valleys.

North America

Europe

South America

Africa

UNDERWATER MOUNTAIN

Most islands are really the peaks of underwater volcanic mountains. Movements in the earth's crust can produce heat and pressure inside an underwater volcano. The pressure eventually causes the volcano to "blow its top." Lava, dust, and rocks flow out, covering the volcano layer by layer, until it breaks the ocean surface and makes an island.

Sea Level

Crust

Mantle

ECHO MEASURE

To measure the ocean's depth, scientists transmit sonar (sound) pulses toward the sea floor, then listen for the echo. The longer it takes to hear the echo, the deeper the water.

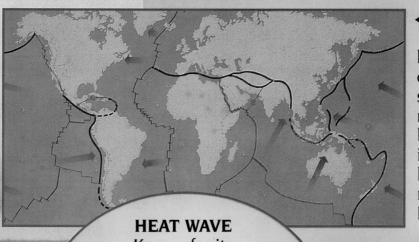

Beneath the seawater and land are pieces of the earth's crust known as plates. In some places on the seafloor, mountains and valleys have been formed by movements in the plates. The largest valley is the Mariana Trench, near the Philippine Islands. It is almost 7 miles deep.

HEAT WAVE
Known for its earthquakes and volcanic eruptions, the "Ring of Fire" is a 24,000-mile circle of volcanoes in the Pacific Ocean. (Above, the "ring" and other volcanoes are represented by small orange dots.)

This deep-sea submersible is exploring the Caribbean.

←— **Volcano**

←— **Shallow Magma Chamber**

←— **Rising Magma**

Deep Source of Magma

FAMOUS PROJECT
When submersibles were used to explore the Ring of Fire in 1974, scientists discovered huge rock chimneys venting clouds of scalding hot water!

21

TO THE BOTTOM

In previous centuries, seagoing merchants had to fight off pirates, who raided and sank ships the world over. A great deal of loot was lost to the sea. Back then, no one could dive into deep waters to retrieve the treasures. Today, however, the right equipment can get an explorer almost anywhere.

About 170 feet below the surface of the sea, scientists explored a 3,400-year-old shipwreck. Among the finds were pottery, bronze weapons, and gold.

HARD HATS
In 1819 Augustus Siebe invented a copper diving helmet (weighing 20 pounds) that allowed divers to reach depths of 200 feet. A long hose, which stretched from the helmet to a pump on the surface, brought air to the diver.

AQUA LUNG
Scuba divers wear tanks containing air, which is fed into the diver's mouthpiece. This breathing device, called the *Aqua Lung*, was developed by Jacques Cousteau, the famous French oceanographer, and Emile Gagnan in 1943. It allows divers to explore the sea as deep as 500 feet.

▲ BRAVE MR. BEEBE
American explorer Charles Beebe was the first to descend to depths no diver could reach. He designed a spherical steel vessel called a bathyscape that could be lowered from a ship by a long cable. In 1934 he reached a depth of 3,028 feet!

DEEP BREATHS

In the deep sea, explorers must wear jointed metal suits that are heavy enough to withstand great water pressure. This kind of atmospheric suit makes it possible for a diver to walk on the sea bottom 2,000 feet below the surface. At right, the submersible *Star* II and the atmospheric diving suit known as JIM take divers to the bottom.

◀SEA LAB

Because underwater living would provide a unique view of the sea, a number of scientists have become *aquanauts*, forsaking land for a few weeks to be with the fishes. With the help of atmospheric suits, vehicles, and robots, the sea may become known in the future as the marine biologist's laboratory.

RECORD DEPTHS

Swiss physicist Auguste Piccard modified the bathyscape so that it could go even deeper. His son Jacques set the record in 1960, when he explored the Mariana Trench, 35,800 feet, almost 7 miles under the sea.

ROBOTIC EXPLORERS

Today, robot submersibles, which can descend 12,000 feet, are used to salvage treasure and explore the sea. In 1985 the *Argo* located the shipwrecked remains of the great ocean liner the *Titanic* (above), which sank in 1912. Its brother robot, *Jason*, was used to explore the wreck.

23

MYSTERIES OF THE DEEP

In 1872, the *Challenger* expedition of British oceanographers proved beyond a doubt that there was life deep down in the ocean. Using scoops and dredges attached to ropes, they gathered samples of 4,417 new marine organisms! But scientists have only recently begun to fathom the mysteries of the deep.

◀ The gulper fish has a huge mouth for swallowing large prey.

▼ This hatchetfish is being pursued by the viperfish (lower right), another deep-sea creature with light organs.

CLIFF HANGER

At a certain distance from each continent, the ocean floor drops sharply to a depth of 20,000 feet. In the very deep sea there is no sunlight, no plants, and the water is icy cold. Below a depth of 7,000 feet in any ocean, the temperature never rises above 39°F!

VOLCANIC CREATURES

Deep down on the ocean floor are vents that spew out scalding hot water. Warmed by liquid rock inside the earth, these springs are rich in minerals. Giant clams, tube worms twelve feet long, and blind crabs and shrimp the size of small dogs, all live near hot-water vents. They eat a special bacteria that manufactures its own food from the vent's gases and heat.

◀ **NIGHT VISION**
Fish in the deep sea are specially adapted to the darkness in which they live. The anglerfish, which glows in the dark, has its own "rod and bait." On the rod are lights that attract prey. A second set of teeth in the back of its throat prevent prey from escaping.

Giant tube worms

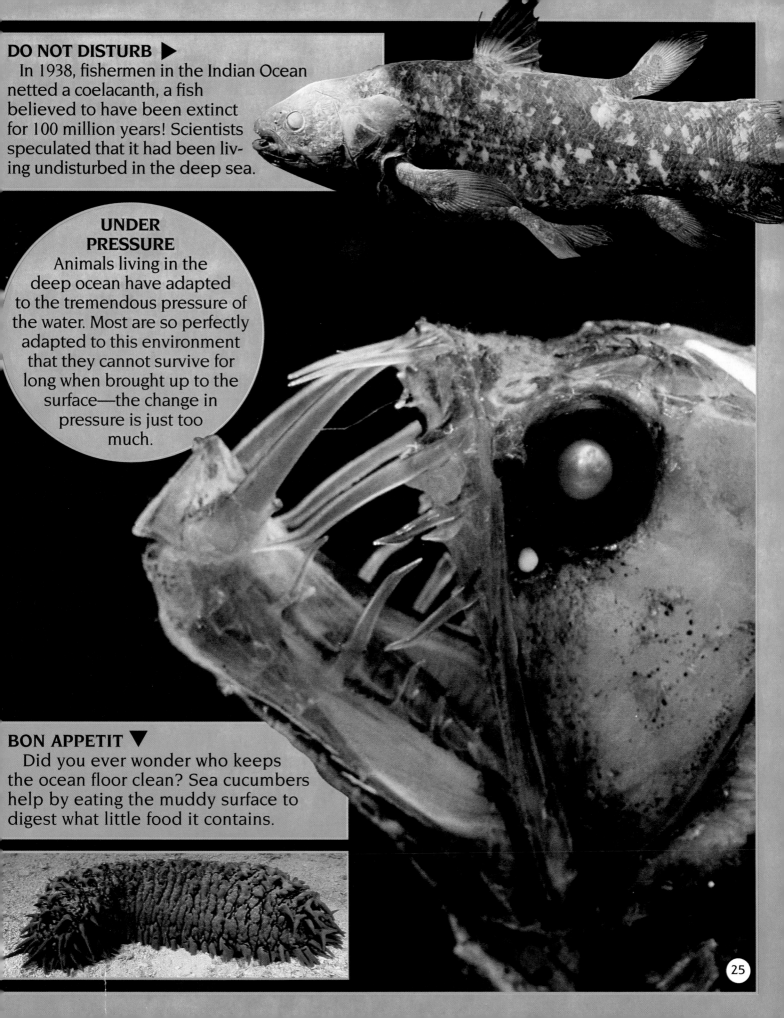

DO NOT DISTURB ▶

In 1938, fishermen in the Indian Ocean netted a coelacanth, a fish believed to have been extinct for 100 million years! Scientists speculated that it had been living undisturbed in the deep sea.

UNDER PRESSURE

Animals living in the deep ocean have adapted to the tremendous pressure of the water. Most are so perfectly adapted to this environment that they cannot survive for long when brought up to the surface—the change in pressure is just too much.

BON APPETIT ▼

Did you ever wonder who keeps the ocean floor clean? Sea cucumbers help by eating the muddy surface to digest what little food it contains.

POLAR WATERS

Have you ever been on top of the world? How about the bottom? They are pretty cold places. The North and South poles, or the Arctic and Antarctica, are known for their icebergs, glaciers, extreme weather, and polar wildlife. They also have a reputation for being dangerous to explorers!

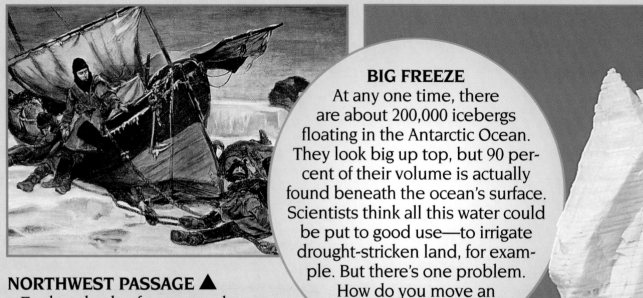

BIG FREEZE

At any one time, there are about 200,000 icebergs floating in the Antarctic Ocean. They look big up top, but 90 percent of their volume is actually found beneath the ocean's surface. Scientists think all this water could be put to good use—to irrigate drought-stricken land, for example. But there's one problem. How do you move an iceberg?

NORTHWEST PASSAGE ▲

For hundreds of years, explorers tried to find a route along the northern coast of Canada which would link the Atlantic to the Pacific Ocean. Searching for the Northwest Passage was dangerous. Ships became frozen into the ice, or were wrecked on icebergs. A route was finally discovered in the 1850s.

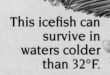

This icefish can survive in waters colder than 32°F.

KEEPING WARM

What would you do to keep warm if you lived in a polar sea? Icefish, and some other polar animals, have special chemicals in their blood that prevent their body's fluids from freezing. Mammals such as whales, seals, and walruses have layers of fat, called blubber, to insulate them from harsh temperatures.

The beluga whale lives in shallow Arctic coastal waters. ▶

A KNACK FOR KAYAK

The Inuits, or Eskimos, developed the kayak— a variation on the canoe, constructed from driftwood and stretched sealskins—to hunt walrus and other Arctic animals. Today's kayaks are fiberglass, and they are paddled all over the world, not just in the Arctic!

POLAR POPULATION

Penguins live in the Antarctic. Polar bears and walruses live in the Arctic. Seals, orcas, and most whales live at both poles. In the winter, seals and walruses hunt under the ice. Seals make holes in the ice where they come up for air.

BOUNTY OF THE SEA

Treasures in the sea are not limited to those lost in shipwrecks. The ocean is a source for food, energy, and valuable minerals.

◀ Salt has been mined from the sea since ancient times.

HOMEMADE JEWELS

What happens when a grain of sand finds its way into a mollusk, such as an oyster or a conch? In one mollusk out of ten thousand, the sand becomes coated with layers of *nacre*, the stuff that forms the shell's shiny insides.

Several years later a pearl is formed! To improve the odds of getting more perfect pearls, people culture the gems themselves, implanting a "seed" in an oyster around which a pearl may grow.

OIL BELOW ▶

Offshore oil wells supply about 17 percent of the world's petroleum. Most rigs are in shallow water, but deep-sea drilling techniques are being developed that could double or triple world production.

HYDRO HEAT

Looking for new energy sources, scientists are developing a new process using seawater. The heat absorbed from the sun could be stored in the water and converted into electricity.

▲ WHAT A CATCH!

A modern fisher's catch consists of fishes that swim in schools, such as tuna, salmon, anchovies, and sardines; fishes that keep to the sea floor, such as cod, haddock, and flounder; and shellfish that are harvested from shallow waters, such as oysters, clams, scallops, and lobsters.

WHALE WATCHING

In the 19th century, more than 70,000 Americans worked in the whaling industry. Whales were hunted to near extinction for their oil and other parts. Whale watching, a new popular million-dollar industry, encourages people to think ecologically.

Fishers break holes in the ice to hook passing fish.

GONE FISHING

In prehistoric times, fishers used sharpened bones for hooks, and vines for fishing line. Modern fishing fleets are like floating factories. Huge trawlers can haul in tons of fishes with each giant net. The catch is then cleaned and quick-frozen at sea.

In Mexico, these fishermen cast a net for their catch.

ENDANGERED OCEAN

All the waters of the world are connected. If one sea, or even one link in the food chain is damaged, people will also be affected. For that reason, pollution could be the real-life sea monster of the modern age.

Sewage dumped along coastlines can produce deadly bacteria in our drinking water and seafood.

DISASTER!

Oil and water don't mix, so an oil spill can spread and cover hundreds of square miles. When the *Exxon Valdez* tanker ran aground in Alaska in 1989, dumping 10 million gallons of oil, it killed hundreds of thousands of marine animals.

Workers attempt to clean up ▶ the oil spilled by a tanker.

POISONED WATER

Rain washes pesticides and fertilizers from farmers' fields and homeowners' lawns into the sea, causing algae to grow out of control and destroy other living things, such as turtles and shellfish. Poisonous emissions from factory chimneys travel through the air and fall upon the land or sea as "acid rain."

CLEAN IT UP!

What is to be done about pollution in the ocean? Enforcing tough laws is a place to start. The Clean Water Act of 1977 mandates controls and cleanups for industrial and municipal pollution. Federal safety regulations, imposed by the U.S. Congress after the *Exxon Valdez* oil spill, assign cleanup costs to oil companies.

FISH FARM

Due to advances in technology, the ocean is in danger of being over-fished. The solution may be *aquaculture*—fish farming. After they hatch from eggs, the fish are fattened up in pens until "harvest time."

The unintentional killing of other sea creatures during shrimping adds to the problem of overfishing the ocean.

A modern fish farm

SAVE THE DOLPHINS!

The fishing nets used to trap tuna often catch dolphins and other marine life, such as the shark shown above. Concern over the many dolphins killed caused major tuna canneries to stop buying tuna caught in nets. Ecologically-minded fishers use hooks instead.

MAN OF THE SEA

By exploring, scientists are learning more about the sea and the marine life it supports. One of the greatest ocean explorers was Jacques Cousteau (1910-1997). He made award-winning documentaries and wrote many books about his discoveries so that others could experience the beauty of this vast underwater realm.

IN NATURE'S PATH

Sometimes the beautiful, serene natural world unleashes its fury. It sets pelting rain, blinding snow, spinning tornadoes, massive hurricanes, rumbling earthquakes, and violent volcanic eruptions upon our glorious planet. Brace yourself as you learn about what can happen to anyone and anything caught in nature's path!

IN NATURE'S PATH

Earthquakes, tornadoes, floods—these are some of the severe acts of nature that affect our planet. What exactly makes them disasters? They are destructive, causing untold hardship and claiming thousands of lives every year.

TOP TWISTER

Tornadoes are spinning winds created by thunderstorms. Often called twisters, they come about when cool, dry air collides with warm, damp air. The Great Tri-State Tornado of March 18, 1925, was the deadliest ever in the U.S. It tore through Missouri, Illinois, and Indiana, killing 695 people.

▲When the Earth quakes, the ground bursts apart.

Approximate location of Earth's plates and the Ring of Fire.

◀ SHAKY GROUND

Both earthquakes and volcanoes are part of the Earth's behavior. Our planet's surface is a rocky crust made up of a dozen or so plates. The plates move, sometimes causing such pressure that the land quakes, especially in an area of the Pacific known as the Ring of Fire. Other times, liquid rock can come up through spaces between the plates, forming a volcano.

SNOWBOUND ▶

A big snowstorm or blizzard can cause a lot of damage and shut a city down. However, snow can be fun and some people make the most of it.

◀ $$$

Hurricanes are formed from tropical storms. Unlike tornadoes, the winds of a hurricane can destroy a broad area and can last for days. Hurricane Andrew was one of the costliest in U.S. history, causing over $46 billion in damage. The storm left over 258,000 people homeless and tore through much of the Everglades National Park.

▼ BURN UP

Dry weather and soaring temperatures often make conditions in the western United States perfect for forest fires.

TO THE RESCUE ▶

Is there anything reassuring in the face of natural disasters? There is often a warning. Forecasters have modern technology at their fingertips—computers, satellites, radar, and more. Also, when a disaster does strike, people come together and help each other out, and professionals come to the rescue—firefighters, medical workers, and special disaster teams.

◀ RAGING RIVER

When it rains, and it pours, it sometimes floods. Imagine two months of rain, and the mighty Mississippi River overflowing its banks. In 1993, nine states in the Midwest experienced the costliest flood in U.S. history —$20 billion in damage was done and about 70,000 people were left homeless.

35

EXPLODING GIANTS

Volcanoes are sometimes called sleeping giants. They can rest quietly for decades or even centuries. But when they wake up, watch out!

OVER THE TOP

The deadliest volcano ever to erupt blew its stack in Sumbawa, Indonesia, in April 1815. Lava and gases killed 92,000 people.

▲ A volcanic ball of fire.

BLAST FROM THE PAST!

One of the biggest volcanic explosions ever recorded took place on an island in Indonesia. On August 27, 1883, Krakatau volcano erupted, killing more than 36,000 people and destroying about 160 villages. It is estimated that the explosion was over 25 times more powerful than the largest hydrogen bomb ever tested!

HOT STUFF ▶

Hot liquid rock erupts from inside the Earth. There, in a layer known as the mantle, temperatures reach a roaring 2,200°F! The thick flowing rock substance is known as magma. Once magma comes out of the ground, it's called lava.

An eruption of ▶ Kilauea in Hawaii.

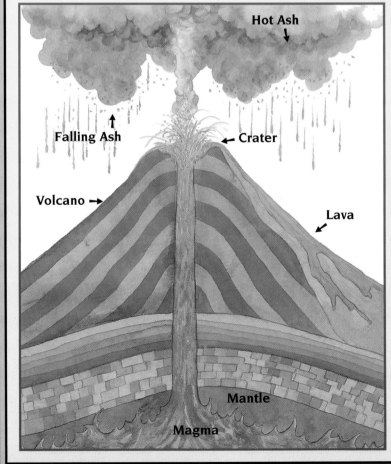

Hot Ash

Falling Ash

Crater

Volcano ➤

Lava

Mantle

Magma

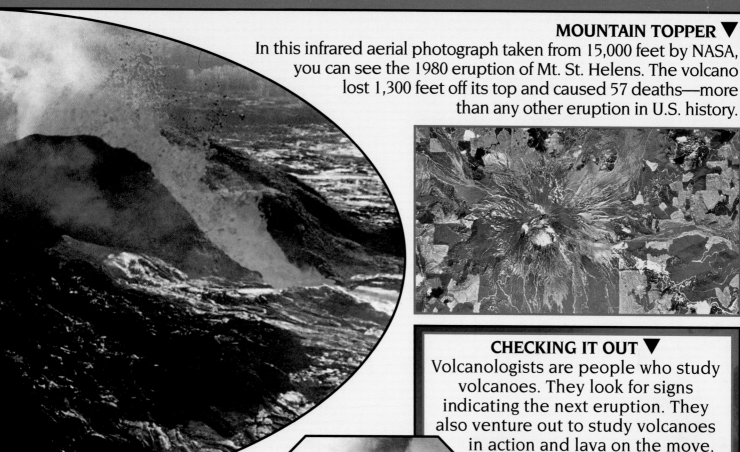

MOUNTAIN TOPPER ▼

In this infrared aerial photograph taken from 15,000 feet by NASA, you can see the 1980 eruption of Mt. St. Helens. The volcano lost 1,300 feet off its top and caused 57 deaths—more than any other eruption in U.S. history.

CHECKING IT OUT ▼

Volcanologists are people who study volcanoes. They look for signs indicating the next eruption. They also venture out to study volcanoes in action and lava on the move.

SAVED BY THE CELL

About 30,000 people died in the eruption of Mt. Pelée on the island of Martinique in the West Indies in 1902. But many people survived. One was spared because the thick walls of his jail cell protected him from the blast.

▼ LAVA WILL TRAVEL

Lava stopped short of these homes near Mt. Etna in Sicily, Italy, and spared them from complete ruin. But lava can really move, swallowing whole cities and destroying all in its path.

▲ These Hollywood cameramen happened to be near-by when a volcano in Mexico erupted in 1943.

GOOD DEEDS

Although volcanoes do damage, they also cause soil to become more fertile and create entire islands, such as Hawaii and Iceland. Also, there are useful volcanic materials, such as pumice and basalt.

LOST CITIES

Almost 2,000 years ago in a Roman city known as Pompeii, a great disaster was about to happen. On the outskirts of town was Mt. Vesuvius. Many people lived near this lovely volcanic mountain. Some farmed its land. Little did they know that the volcano was ready to blow its top!

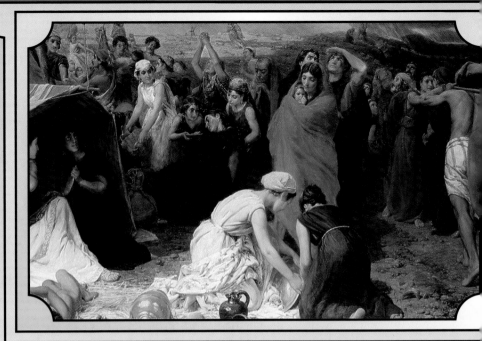

▲ BLOW UP

On August 24, A.D. 79, Mt. Vesuvius erupted. Within hours, Pompeii was buried under 6 to 20 feet of ash and spongy rock, called pumice. Forgotten, Herculaneum was destroyed by a super hot river of lava. Both cities were not to be discovered for many centuries.

▼ STOPPED DEAD IN THEIR TRACKS

People from Pompeii were buried as they tried to escape. Over the years as they deteriorated, the bodies left a space in the hardened volcanic rock. Archaeologists (scientists who study past cultures) discovered these spaces and poured liquid plaster down into the rock. They later dug out the hardened plaster, creating a permanent record of the fallen victims.

◄VIEW OF VESUVIUS

Vesuvius has been painted by many artists. This painting depicts people fleeing Pompeii. Citizens who actually survived the rain of volcanic ash returned to their city to scavenge for riches. In later centuries people continued to pillage, and many archaeological treasures ended up in museums.

▲ A house in Pompeii.

◄ In Pompeii, the ovens from a baker's shop survived the volcanic eruption.

LOST AND FOUND

Houses and other buildings have been uncovered in Pompeii and Herculaneum, leaving a perfect time capsule of daily life almost 2,000 years ago. However, much remains to be excavated in Herculaneum. Work there has been more difficult than at Pompeii, because Herculaneum was buried in lava, which is much heavier than ash and pumice.

▲ The house of Poseidon in Herculaneum contains the best-known mosaic discovered in the ruins.

LOOKS CAN FOOL

Look out! Mt. Vesuvius can erupt again. It is, after all, an active volcano. An active volcano is one that is erupting or has erupted since the time that written records have been kept. The last really spectacular eruption of Mt. Vesuvius occurred in 1944, and in 1906 the volcano blew off the ring of its crater.

◄ Mt. Vesuvius and the remains of Pompeii in present-day southern Italy.

39

QUAKES

Like much of nature's fury, earthquakes are short-lived. But their destruction echoes for years. Earthquakes have been taking place since the beginning of time. And although scientists are better able to predict them today, earthquakes still cause enormous damage and great loss of life.

Part of this house broke away during the 1994 earthquake in Los Angeles.

PURE DESTRUCTION

The Los Angeles earthquake of January 17, 1994, was the most destructive in U.S. history, killing 61 people and injuring more than 8,000. The loss in dollars was close to $20 billion.

DEFINITELY DEADLY
Fortunately, some earthquakes hit where few people live and work. Others, however, offer no such mercy. One of these deadly quakes occurred in Tangshan, China, in 1976. Registering 8.2 on the Richter scale, the quake killed 242,000 people!

▲ Workers rescued this man from a collapsed building after the 1994 quake in California.

DOUBLE-TEAMING

The strongest earthquake in U.S. history struck Prince William Sound, Alaska, on March 27, 1964. It measured 9.2 on the Richter scale. Following the quake came a giant wave, called a tsunami (soo-NAH-me). The wave, which traveled at 450 mph, destroyed the town of Kodiak.

This geologist is examining a seismograph after an earthquake measuring 5.0 hit Los Angeles. The machine records movements in the Earth.

◀ A quake does more than shake the Earth. It breaks open water lines and brings down power lines, causing fires and floods.

HELPING HANDS

After the disastrous earthquake in Armenia on December 7, 1988, was reported on television, rescue workers from all over the world came to help. The quake, measuring 6.9 on the Richter scale, killed over 25,000 people, injured 15,000, and left 400,000 homeless.

TAKING MEASURE

Charles F. Richter invented what is known as the Richter scale. It has been used since 1935 to measure the strength of an earthquake. Very few earthquakes register above an 8.0. If one does, it means there's a whole lot of shaking going on!

JAPAN'S HORROR

Located on the Ring of Fire, where four out of five earthquakes occur, Japan gets hit hard by quakes. On January 17, 1995, a quake struck Kobe with a magnitude of 7.2 on the Richter scale, causing about $100 billion in damage.

◀ On September 1, 1923, an earthquake struck the Kanto Plain in Japan, leaving over 550,000 dwellings destroyed.

41

SHAKY SAN FRANCISCO

San Francisco, California, is a fun place to visit. There are cable cars and neat hills, a blue bay, and, beyond it, the Pacific Ocean. But, unless you like living on the edge, you may not want to live there. Sometimes tremors occur and there's little destruction. But when a big quake hits, the effects can be disastrous.

▶ Between quakes, the city enjoys a quiet, peaceful time.

▼ Search teams use dogs to find people trapped in the rubble of collapsed buildings.

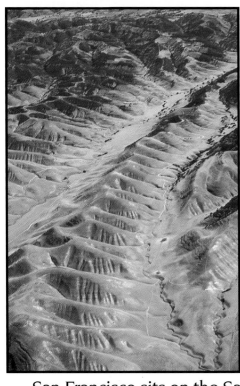

The San Andreas fault lines.

A MAJOR FAULT

San Francisco sits on the San Andreas fault—a 600-mile stretch where a crack exists in the Earth's crust. When the huge plates that make up the crust push into each other, and the colliding rocks can no longer bend, the Earth begins to tremble under the pressure and an earthquake occurs.

Fires following the 1906 quake roared out of control, as the city's main water supply was cut off.

CITY IN CHAOS

In the San Francisco earthquake of April 18, 1906, more than 500 people died and over four square miles of buildings were destroyed.

Hotels, hospitals, and other buildings collapsed.

TWISTERS

Their swirling winds spin at speeds of 250 miles per hour or more, picking up anything in their paths, including cars and trains. Tornadoes can snap telephone poles like twigs and peel the roofs off of houses, tossing them like Frisbees.

WHAT IS IT?

It's a twister, a cyclone, a whirlwind! All these words are used for a tornado, the storm with the fastest and strongest winds on Earth. But what *is* a tornado? It's a violently rotating column of air produced by a thunderstorm. Funnel shaped, the vortex usually moves over the land in a narrow path, staying in contact with both the thundercloud and the ground.

When a twister contacts water instead of the ground, it forms a waterspout.

ONSTAGE

Between April 3 and 4, in 1974, over 140 tornadoes touched down in 13 states and Canada. It was a lucky day, however, for some drama students at the local high school in Xenia, Ohio. They escaped to a hallway just in time—before two buses landed onstage.

◀ Destruction to Xenia

44

Most tornadoes in the U.S. occur in the Midwest. Kansas, Missouri, Oklahoma, and Texas make up a region known as Tornado Alley. Oklahoma is struck by tornadoes more than any other place on Earth.

LISTEN UP

Tornado season occurs in both spring and fall. If heavy thunderstorms are in your area, turn on your TV or radio. A tornado *watch* means that the thunderstorms could contain tornadoes. A tornado *warning* means that a tornado has actually been detected on radar or seen by people.

WHAT TO DO WHEN A TWISTER HITS

How do you stay safe when a tornado is hurling a barn from its foundation or stripping the roof off a house? Some people have fiberglass shelters buried in their backyards. Others take refuge in the basement.

OFF THE CHARTS

Tornadoes are rated from F0 to F5 based on the damage they do. A rating of F0 means that the damage was light. Maybe some windows were shattered. A rating of F5 means that the damage was "incredible," with houses and cars carried away. The scale, called the Fujita scale, was devised by T. Theodore Fujita, a physics professor.

An F2 can rip the roof off a house.

HURRICANES

They kill more people than any other storms. They uproot trees, flatten buildings, and cause floods. With winds of up to 220 mph, they devastate entire cities. Andrew, Camille, Agnes, and Gilbert—these are the names given to some of the most devastating hurricanes in history.

High tides caused by Hurricane Marilyn ▶ carried boats onto the streets in the Virgin Islands.

Much of the damage from hurricanes is caused by huge ocean waves blown to shore.

1954

It was not a good year for people living along the Eastern seaboard. In August, Hurricane Carol pounded the area. In October, Hurricane Hazel tore through the country, hitting Canada as well.

WHAT'S IN A NAME?

Hurricanes used to have only female names. But since 1979, hurricanes have been named for men and women. The first man's name to be used was Bob.

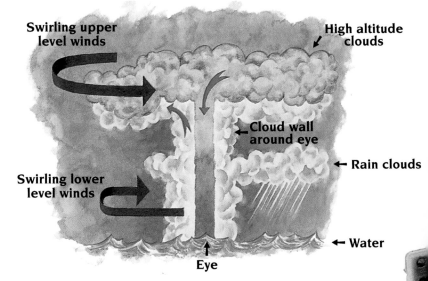

Swirling upper level winds

High altitude clouds

Cloud wall around eye

← Rain clouds

Swirling lower level winds

← Water

Eye

▲ BIG WIND

Hurricanes form over the ocean when warm air combines with cool air to create wind. If water is present and the wind is strong, a tropical storm forms. About half these storms become hurricanes.

INSIDE THE EYE ▶

A hurricane has a calm center, called an eye, which you can see in this satellite image of Hurricane Gilbert. Satellites help forecasters give early warning to residents and, therefore, help save lives. But satellites weren't around in 1900, when a hurricane hit Galveston, Texas, and killed 6,000. It was the worst hurricane disaster in the U.S.

FAST AND FURIOUS

In 1969, winds of Hurricane Camille reached 200 mph—the fastest sustained winds in a U.S. hurricane—as they pounded Mississippi and Louisiana.

▼ ALSO KNOWN AS

Hurricanes are called typhoons in the China seas and cyclones in the Indian Ocean. Regardless, they're usually deadly. Typhoon Ike devastated the Southern Philippines on September 2, 1984. More than 1,300 people died in flash floods triggered by the storm.

A ▶ U.S. soldier helps a young girl and her family get emergency supplies after Hurricane Andrew destroyed their home in Florida in 1992.

▲ Wreckage from Hurricane Hugo.

IT'S SNOWING!

Snowflakes cover trees, lawns, buildings, cars, and roads with a clean-looking velvety blanket. What could be more enchanting? But snow can also be dangerous. When a light dusting turns into a storm, which turns into a blizzard, few people are thinking about beauty.

BLANKET OF WHITE

The most disastrous winter storm in U.S. history took place in 1888. For about four days, a blizzard dropped five feet of snow all along the East Coast. Over 400 people died, and damage was estimated at about $20 million.

Wind is part of the problem during a blizzard. It piles snow in drifts and makes it difficult for people to navigate through city streets or over country roads.

BOWL OF SNOW

The greatest snowfall in a single storm in North America occurred at California's Mt. Shasta Ski Bowl from February 13 to 19, 1959. Over 15 feet of white stuff fell. That's over twice the height of basketball star Shaquille O'Neal.

SUPER-COOL ART ▶

People always rise to the occasion when nature sends mountains of flakes. If conditions are not disastrous, some people like to make snowmen or go sledding or skiing. Then there are the more serious creative types. Here, an artist in chilly Minnesota gets down to business sculpting a face of snow three stories high.

48

◄ AVALANCHE

An avalanche is an uncontrollable slide of ice and snow traveling hundreds of miles per hour. A volcano can cause an avalanche. The Mt. Saint Helens eruption on May 18, 1980, in Washington, caused 96 billion cubic feet of snow to go tumbling down.

▼ A snow-covered Mt. Saint Helens.

In 1947, traffic was at a standstill during one of the worst blizzards ever to hit New York City.

▼ RECORD BREAKER

Unusual for New York City, streets were almost completely empty on January 8, 1996. The blizzard that hit caused the entire Northeast to come to a near stand-still. Schools were closed and businesses were shut tight.

In 1996, New York broke its 1947 record of 63.2 inches of total snowfall in one year with a chilling 75.6 inches.

FIRE!

It's true that people cause a lot of forest fires. Matches get thrown down on the dry forest floor, or a campfire is not extinguished properly. But nature sets its own fires, especially when the land is dry and the wind is blowing. In July 1994, in the western U.S., conditions were perfect for a fire. Lightning ignited trees, setting off a blaze that caused 240,000 acres to burn in 11 states. Fourteen firefighters died near Glenwood Springs, Colorado.

TALK ABOUT HOT!

It was 1871, the driest year in memory, and small fires were burning all over Wisconsin. Some got way out of control. In the forest fire that burned in Peshtigo, on October 8, 1871, about 1,200 lives were lost. Over 1 million acres burned in what is considered the worst U.S. forest fire in history.

SMOKEY

His official name is Smokey the Bear. His official slogan is "Only *you* can prevent forest fires." In 1968, Smokey had become the most popular symbol in the U.S., beating out President Lyndon B. Johnson.

IN THE WOODS

In California, some homes are so close to the woods and forests that fires often overtake them. From October 20 to 23, 1991, a brush fire in Oakland destroyed over 3,000 homes and apartments, causing about $1.5 billion in damage.

LENDING A HAND

Over 10,000 fire-fighters from all over the United States came to help put out the 1988 fire in Yellowstone National Park. They cleared parts of the forest to create firebreaks, areas where there would be nothing the fire could feed on. But strong winds kept pushing the flames across the breaks.

GOOD AND BAD

Some feel that forest fires may actually be a blessing. As the forest floor gets cluttered with underbrush and fallen trees, a potential fire becomes more and more dangerous. A fire tends to clean up the area and enables new trees to grow. And although wildlife flees the area during the time of danger, animals return once the fire is out.

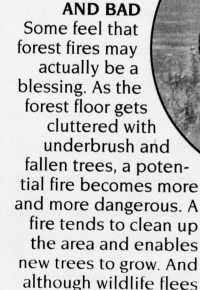

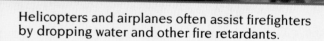

Helicopters and airplanes often assist firefighters by dropping water and other fire retardants.

▼ WALL OF FIRE

Yellowstone, one of the largest national parks in the United States, has over 2.2 million acres. In the summer of 1988, over 1.3 million acres burned—more than half the park! It was the worst forest fire in any of our national parks.

▲ Flooding in northern California reached the roofs in 1995.

FIERCE FLOODS

Rain is an essential part of our world. But when there's too much, we get floods and a number of other disastrous events. Rivers overflow and take houses and cars with them. Power lines go down, and fires get started. Then, mud may slide over the land.

During the flood in the Midwest in 1993, which left thousands of people homeless, farm animals and pets had to be rescued, too.

▲ Firemen are rescuing a man who went back to his flooded home in St. Louis to rescue his cat.

▼ The airport in Jefferson City, Missouri, was completely covered by water in the 1993 flood.

BROKEN DAM ▶
More than 2,200 people died in the Johnstown, Pennsylvania, flood of 1889—one of the worst floods in U.S. history. A dam broke, causing a 20-to-30-foot-high wall containing 20 million tons of water to careen through Little Conemaugh Valley.

IMPERFECTION
Almost a century after the Johnstown flood of 1889, a new flood-control system was in place. It was declared practically perfect. Not so! Another flood swept over the land on July 19, 1977.

DANGEROUS RIVER
Southeast Asia experiences a lot of flooding. The Yellow River in China has overflowed many times. Major flooding there has caused the death of millions. In one flood alone, in 1931, 3.7 million people died.

IN A FLASH
Flash floods occur after heavy rains when the weather has been dry. This downpour causes lakes and reservoirs to overflow. Dry ground can't absorb the runoff fast enough.

In 1995, heavy rains flooded many European cities.

NATURAL PHENOMENA

When you think of natural disasters, you may think of earthquakes shaking down houses, floods covering the land, or tornadoes carrying off property. But there are other phenomena with weird and disastrous results.

A landslide buried this town in the Philippines after a volcanic eruption.

◀ Workers wade through a muddy volcanic aftermath in Colombia.

Heavy rains in California in 1995 created disastrous mudslides.

LANDSLIDE

Too much rain can turn soil to mud, and too much creates a landslide. Landslides can also be caused by earthquakes, which loosen rock and debris.

These kids have captured a few giant hailstones from a recent storm.

INCREDIBLE ICE BALLS

Sometimes perfect balls of ice, hail is one of those strange things in nature we're sometimes excited to see. But hail can be dangerous. In 1990, 60 people were injured by baseball-size hailstones in Colorado. It was a costly hailstorm, causing over $625 million in damage.

▼ REALLY BAD LUCK

Imagine being struck by lightning once. Disaster! Now imagine being struck by lightning seven times—and living to tell the tales. Former park ranger Roy C. Sullivan was struck in 1942 for the first time. Then, he was hit again in 1969, 1970, 1972, 1973, 1976, and 1977.

▲ WHALE OF A GALE

What is not a tornado or hurricane, but is not just a breeze? Strong winds known as gales. They shake whole trees and make it difficult for people to walk. These Japanese tourists got caught off guard in Paris by gusts of winds traveling over 80 mph!

▼ One of many famous photographs taken of the dust bowl. Photographer Arthur Rothstein captured a father and his children running for cover as a storm of dust approached.

DUST BOWL

What happens when you don't have rain? Drought. The longest drought of the 20th century took place in the U.S. in the 1930s. During 1934, dry regions stretched from New York to California. Much of the Great Plains was called the "dust bowl." There, topsoil blew away easily because it had been overworked. Strong winds carried it around and created drifts of fine dust.

WHAT A DEVIL!

Tornadoes suck up anything in their path. When they travel over the desert, sand is the thing they pick up most. This swirl of grit is called a dust devil, and its name suits it.

SCIENCE OLD AND NEW

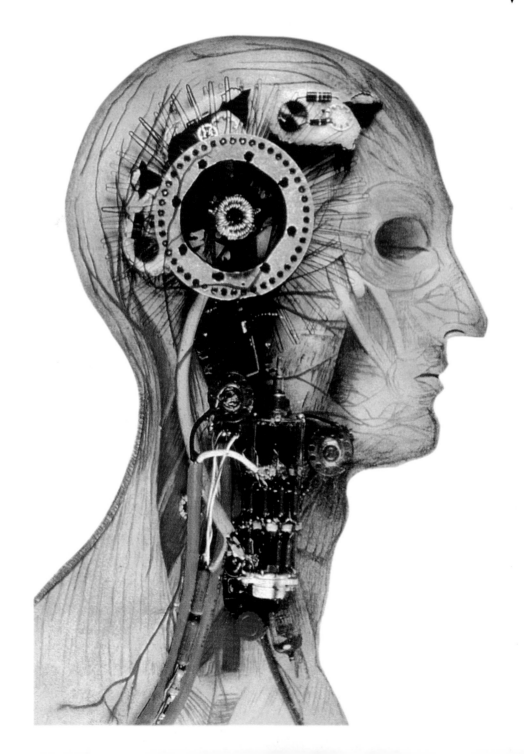

For thousands of years, scientists have explored and studied our world and the wonders of what may lie beyond it. From delving into the tiniest atomic particle to charting the farthest reaches of the universe, science helps us understand the world around us. Get ready to discover the amazing information behind the mysteries and phenomena of our world!

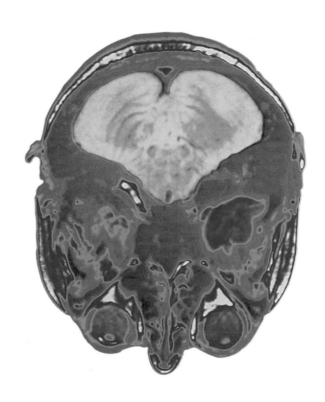

WHAT AN IDEA!

Once upon a time, it would have been as weird to believe that Earth is round as it would be now to believe it is flat. In science, curiosity and the need to solve problems lead to investigation. Then new information and technology can turn strange ideas into reality.

NEW VIEW

In 1609, Galileo looked at the moon through a new invention, the telescope, and saw craters. That may not be a shock to you. But at that time, people believed that Earth was unique, and at the center of the universe. To them, the moon was a heavenly globe of light. But Galileo discovered that the moon is a world that, in some ways, resembles our own. Galileo changed our ideas about the universe forever.

AN INSPIRING BATH ▼

In the 3rd century B.C., Archimedes had a difficult problem to solve—he needed to measure the volume of the king's crown, an irregularly shaped object. As this story is often told, Archimedes solved his problem while taking a bath. Climbing in, Archimedes realized that he was pushing out an amount of water equal to his body's volume. "Eureka!" he cried, meaning "I have it!" All he had to do was put the crown in water and measure the water it displaced.

A SMALL WORLD

Plagues have killed millions throughout history. But before the mid-19th century, no one knew about germs. When Louis Pasteur proved his germ theory, he convinced doctors to boil their instruments and wash their hands. One of medicine's greatest discoveries, it led to a doubling of life expectancy and a population explosion.

This microscope image (shown in background) is the bacteria E. *coli*, which lives naturally in the human intestine and is necessary to a person's good health.

HORSE SENSE ▲

In 1872, two men made a bet about whether all four of a horse's hooves leave the ground when it gallops. To settle the bet, photographer Eadweard Muybridge set up 24 tripwires and cameras along a racetrack. As the horse galloped, it triggered the cameras one after the other. One photo showed all four feet in the air.

CHANGING ▶ TRUTH

Democritus (460-370 B.C.) said that all matter was composed of parti-cles so tiny that nothing smaller was conceivable. He called them atoms, meaning "indivis-ible." Too weird for the time, the idea wasn't taken seriously for 2,000 years. After all, you can't see atoms—250 million of them lined up measure only one inch! Even smaller are the subatomic particles that make up an atom—protons, neutrons, and electrons.

59

IT'S RELATIVE ▲

Albert Einstein changed our view of time. His theory said that if one twin traveled through space while the other stayed on Earth, both twins would feel time pass normally. But time would slow down for the traveling twin, and he would age less than his twin on Earth. An experiment with an atomic clock carried by a jetliner proved Einstein correct. The clock showed less time passing than a clock on Earth.

CURIOUS CURES

Until about 100 years ago, bloodletting was a normal treatment for many illnesses, including fevers and pneumonia. The doctor would cut the patient in a particular area of the body and let a certain amount of blood flow out. Now we think of this as weird, because loss of blood is harmful, not helpful. But some of the treatments we use today seem every bit as strange.

◀ IN THE DIRT

Where do you find wonder drugs? Scientists have poked around in the mud and muck to find them. The organism that produces streptomycin, an important antibiotic, was first discovered on a hen. Scientists then searched the whole farm and found the organism in the heavily manured soil around the henhouse.

OUCH! ▲

It may look painful, but acupuncture is a Chinese medical procedure that actually helps relieve pain. Even pets get relief. The physician may insert needles at more than 360 points in the body, and then twirl the needles or send electrical currents through them. In China, acupuncture is often used along with drugs during brain surgery.

◀ GROSS WORKS

Some ancient remedies are still used today. After reattaching fingers or toes, doctors may apply leeches—blood-sucking worms— to help keep tiny blood vessels from clogging. Maggots are used to remove dead flesh. And physicians sometimes pack deep wounds with the same thing used by Egyptians 4,000 years ago—sugar.

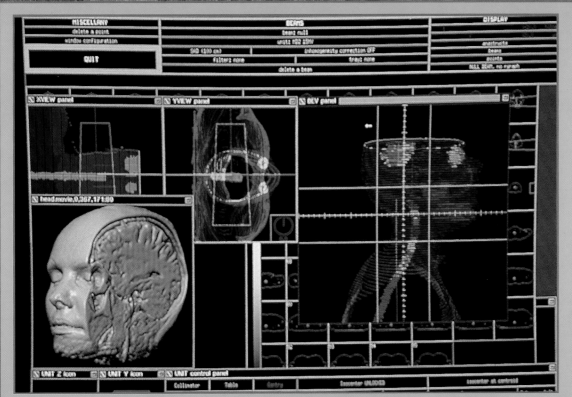

KILL TO HEAL

Although X rays were first observed by accident, scientists have learned much about radiation and put it to good use. Too much radiation can be fatal to humans, but, by focusing those killing powers on diseased cells, radiation can be used to treat cancer.

▲ A computer is used to plan radiation treatment.

GROWING CURES

We often think of plant remedies as something used only by ancient people, but almost 80 percent of people today rely mainly on this traditional medicine. Nearly 50 percent of medicines on the market come from plants. More than 25 percent of all medicines come from ingredients found in rainforest plants and animals.

◀ Marie Curie (1867-1934), the only person to win two Nobel Prizes in science, was the first to describe the process of radiation.

FROG MEDICINE

Long used by Ecuadorian Choco Indians as a weapon, the venom from the poison arrow frog can help as well as hurt. One compound in the venom acts as a painkiller that is 200 times better at fighting pain than morphine, a drug used in hospitals.

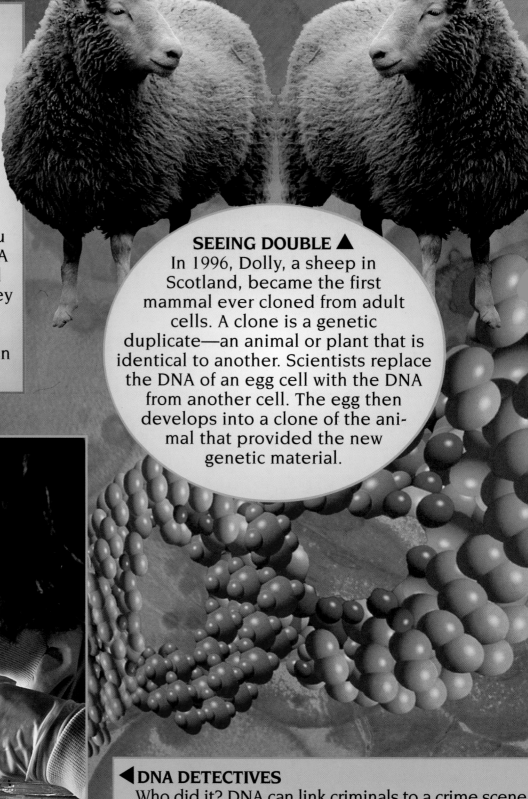

THE GENE SCENE

Our genes carry DNA (deoxyribonucleic acid)—the substance that makes us unique individuals. Although it fits into a single cell, the human DNA molecule is about six feet long. If you stretched out all the DNA molecules in a baby, and put them end to end, they would reach 114 billion miles—thirty times the distance between the Sun and Pluto!

SEEING DOUBLE ▲

In 1996, Dolly, a sheep in Scotland, became the first mammal ever cloned from adult cells. A clone is a genetic duplicate—an animal or plant that is identical to another. Scientists replace the DNA of an egg cell with the DNA from another cell. The egg then develops into a clone of the animal that provided the new genetic material.

◀ DNA DETECTIVES

Who did it? DNA can link criminals to a crime scene better than any fingerprint. Scientists use blood or skin cells found at the scene to create a genetic profile, which they compare to the suspect's. In one case, the DNA taken from cat hairs found at the scene of a crime was matched to that of the suspect's pet. The man was found guilty and convicted.

FAMILY TREES ▼

By using DNA, it's possible to trace family relationships. Scientists studying the DNA of a 9,000-year-old skeleton from Cheddar, England, discovered that he had a living descendant—the local school teacher! That's a family tree with long roots.

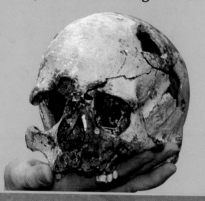

▲ ZONKEY!

What happens when you cross a zebra with a donkey? You get a crossbreed, an offspring with a mix of genes from both parents. Through biotechnology, scientists may isolate a specific gene from one species and give it to another, creating new varieties of plants and animals.

GENE ALARM

Do you wake up at the same time every day? We all have a biological clock that controls our sleep cycle. Researchers have discovered that, in mice, a gene controls this clock.

SAVING SPECIES

Test-tube tigers? Scientists are using frozen sperm and eggs to create baby animals that belong to endangered species. By fertilizing the egg in a test tube, it is possible to breed animals separated by great distances that might not otherwise mate.

▶ DINOS TODAY?

Bad news for *Jurassic Park* fans. In the movie, scientists used DNA taken from blood in the stomachs of biting insects trapped in amber (fossilized tree resin) to re-create dinosaurs. In reality, this would be impossible. However, scientists have discovered some pieces of dinosaur DNA in fossil bones.

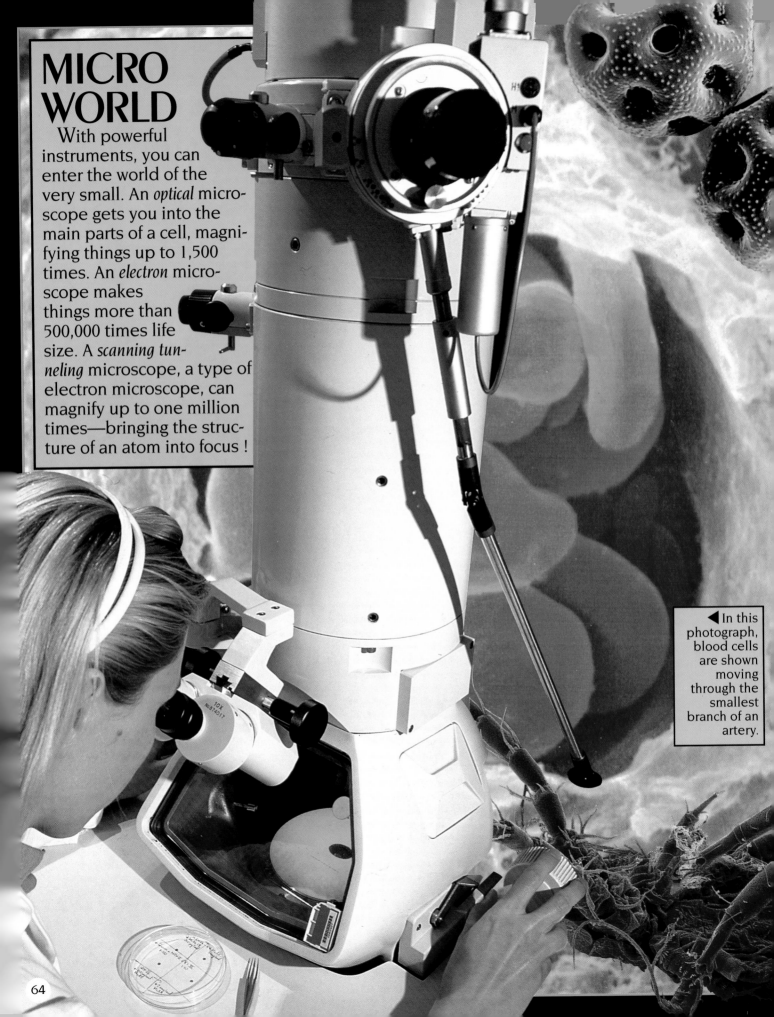

MICRO WORLD

With powerful instruments, you can enter the world of the very small. An *optical* microscope gets you into the main parts of a cell, magnifying things up to 1,500 times. An *electron* microscope makes things more than 500,000 times life size. A *scanning tunneling* microscope, a type of electron microscope, can magnify up to one million times—bringing the structure of an atom into focus!

◄ In this photograph, blood cells are shown moving through the smallest branch of an artery.

10X
NO.874017

▲Pollen can cause allergic reactions known as hayfever.

AH-CHOO!

The body has a remarkable defense against infection. But in some people, this immune system gets a little confused. It recognizes certain harmless particles as dangerous and tries to fight them off. An allergic reaction is the result, which can be minor, like a sneeze, or, in extreme cases, life-threatening.

MICRO WARFARE

Viruses represent one of the biggest challenges to over-coming infectious diseases. When a virus, such as the common cold, invades a cell, it forces the cell to make copies of the virus. To attack the virus is to attack the body's own living cells. No cures exist, only preventive vaccines.

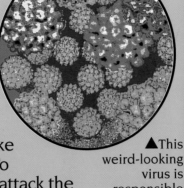

▲This weird-looking virus is responsible for causing warts.

TOUGH GUYS

You think you're tough? Some bacteria live in boiling hot water. Others survive radiation that would kill a human. Scientists have even found bacteria living 4,500 feet below the ground. These bacteria appear to survive in total darkness on nutrients they extract from the rocks.

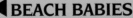

MITE-Y SMALL

You never see them, but the tiny spider relatives known as mites (left) are all around us, even in the cleanest house. They crawl through carpet, prowl your bed, and even live in your hair! But don't confuse them with the blood-sucking, foul-smelling insects known as bedbugs (above). Mites actually help keep your house clean by feeding on flakes of dead skin.

◀ BEACH BABIES

It's just a beach, or is it? Living in the sand is one of the richest animal communities found on Earth. These tiny meiofauna (MY-oh-faw-nah) are strange creatures— some have heads cov-ered with whirling hairs, others cling to sand grains with hooked claws. A single handful of wet sand may hold 10,000 of these animals.

NATURAL ODDITIES

Imagine finding a new life form, or talking to animals. In nature, scientists encounter some pretty strange things, and engineer some weird ways of getting inside an animal's world.

▲DOWN DEEP

In the murky waters of the Amazon River, where light penetrates to only a few inches below the surface, many new species of fish are being discovered. Mostly blind, they rely on electrical signals to navigate the dark river water.

WHITE WONDER▼

Coloration exists for a reason in nature, often as camouflage against predators. That's why it's strange to find an animal colored differently than the norm—like this pure white emperor penguin spotted in Antarctica. Sometimes white animals are albinos, which lack pigment and have red eyes. However, this penguin is not an albino, but a kind of genetic mutant rarely seen.

◀ SPYING CRABS

How do you know if an animal is using its eyes, and not its sense of smell? Some scientists mounted a tiny spy camera above the eyes of a male horseshoe crab to make a film of what the crab saw—female crabs. Meanwhile, they monitored electrical responses in the nerves that connect the eyes to the brain. Back in the lab, male crabs who saw the film responded in much the same way as the crab on the loose, proving that the eyes were at work.

PUPPET MOM ▶

Raising animals in captivity leads to all sorts of trouble. The animals see humans as protective parents and never learn to survive on their own. One solution to raising bald eagles and other birds is to use puppets that look like the adult animals. The babies receive food from a beak, not a human hand.

SMART TALK ▲

Have you ever wondered if animals have their own language? A study on prairie dogs used a computer to correlate squeaks and chirps with events happening at the time. Results suggested that prairie-dog talk distinguishes a coyote from a German shepherd and a man from a woman.

▼ARTY APES

Believe it or not, people can communicate with animals. The famous gorilla named Koko began learning sign language in the 1970s. She uses more than 1,000 signs to relay her thoughts. One of her favorite activities is painting. When asked what her blue, red, and yellow painting was, Koko answered, "bird."

PLANT FIGHT

When disease strikes, plants fight back. At least, that's what some scientists think. Plants produce the chemical salicylic acid, which is found in aspirin, when they are sick. This self-made medicine boosts a plant's immune system. It also stimulates other plants to be on the defense.

LOST IN TIME

When the first fossils were found, no one knew what they were. Fossils are traces of plants and animals preserved in the earth. Today, scientists called paleontologists (pay-lee-on-TALL-oh-jists) are unraveling the stories that fossils tell.

STRANGE CREATURES

Preserved in 530-million-year-old rock in Canada, called the Burgess Shale, are some of the weirdest animals that ever lived on Earth. One was a worm with five eyes and a trunk.

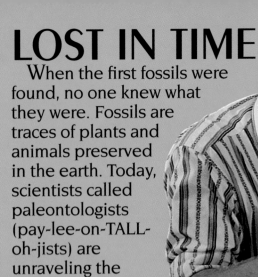

FEATHERED FINDS ▲

A rich fossil bed discovered in China in the 1990s is remarkable because of the amount of detail preserved in the rock. Among its treasures are lots of bird fossils showing feathers, including the oldest beaked bird.

HUGE INHABITANTS ▼

Fossils reveal that South America had some hefty inhabitants—an eight-ton, meat-eating dinosaur we call Giganotosaurus, and the plant-eater Argentinosaurus (below), which weighed in at around 100 tons. Other discoveries include two-foot spiders and a forty-foot-long crocodile.

ANCIENT FOREST

A subtropical forest only 680 miles from the North Pole? On Axel Heiberg Island, scientists found the *mummified* remains of one. The forest grew 45 million years ago when the area was warm and swampy. The really weird thing is that the wood could still burn today.

UP IN THE AIR ▶

If you had been in Texas about 65 million years ago, you might have seen something impressive overhead—the largest flying creature ever, a reptile called Quetzalcoatlus (KWET-zal-KWA-tel-us). It weighed about 190 pounds and had a wingspan of about 40 feet—the size of a small plane.

▼ CYBER DINOS

If you want to see how dinosaurs moved, you have to bring them to life. Some scientists have done just that—in cyber space. They used software to reconstruct sauropods, such as Apatosaurus (also known as Brontosaurus). This 100-ton dino may have broken the sound barrier, creating a sonic boom by using its 3,500-pound tail like a whip!

THE GREAT DYING

The dinosaurs died out 65 million years ago, but about 245 million years ago, a much larger extinction event took place. During what is known as the Great Dying, as much as 96 percent of all plant and animal species on Earth may have been wiped out.

COLORFUL DINO?

Ever wonder what color Stegosaurus really was? Researchers looking at fossils have identified structures and pigments responsible for colors. Using this information, they've determined that a 370-million-year-old fish was dark red on top and silver underneath. Could the dinosaurs be next?

DIGGING HISTORY

Scientists are still trying to piece together human history, especially the prehistoric period when no written language existed and few records were kept. Archaeologists and anthropologists are the detectives looking for the clues.

OLD ART ▲

The last time human eyes saw these cave paintings, discovered in 1994 in the Ardeche River canyon of France, may have been 30,000 years ago. Over 300 paintings represent Ice Age animals that include horses, bears, rhinoceroses, and bison.

▼ MODEL PAST

Starting with a skull and using charts that show the thickness of tissue, scientists can re-create faces from long ago. They build models of the face from clay or use computers to make a three-dimensional image.

JIGSAW HEAD ▲

Bones and artifacts, discovered on a dig or purely by chance, can take scientists back millions of years. Richard Leakey and his team of researchers found 150 skull fragments and other bones in Kenya dating almost 2 million years ago. The team reconstructed the skull, and named it "handy man" because it was found alongside stone tools.

◄ PEKING MAN

A famous collection of fossils known as Peking Man was discovered in 1921 in China. Thought to be 400,000 years old, the bones were the first of their kind found in Asia. Stone tools were also found in the cave.

Did some European explorer beat Columbus to the Americas? The remains of eight buildings and other artifacts discovered in Newfoundland, Canada, in 1960 finally confirmed that Vikings got here long before 1492. But their attempt to settle the continent failed.

ICE MAN
Imagine hiking in the Alps and finding a body that's over 5,000 years old, preserved like a time capsule in a glacier. That's what happened in 1991, when two mountaineers discovered the "Ice Man."

BOG BODIES
In cool places where water stands still, layers of dead plants pile up sometimes 40 feet thick underneath living plants, and a bog is formed. Called peat, the dead plant matter is useful as a kind of fuel. People digging for peat have made some bizarre discoveries. They have found perfectly preserved bodies—whiskers and clothes included—dating from over 2,000 years ago.

HANDLE WITH CARE
Scientists can use high-tech methods to learn all about a mummy without damaging it. Using Computer Assisted Tomography (CAT) scanning, they take a series of X-ray pictures of the mummy still in its wooden case. Then the computer adds up the images to create a 3-D image.

71

SPOOKY SPACE

In the vast reaches of space, almost everything, like the death of a star, seems weird and mysterious. At the end of its life, a star may collapse in upon itself and form a black hole. Sounds interesting, but you don't want to visit. A black hole's gravity is so strong that it pulls in everything around it, even light.

Gas exhaust from this dying star moves in twin jets at a velocity greater than 200 miles per second.

SPACE INVADERS

Earth gets pelted by about 20 tons of rock a day from meteorites, asteroids, and comets. Most of the material arrives as grain-sized particles. Really big impacts that cause widespread destruction occur only about once every 100 million years.

COSMIC SNOWBALLS ▲

Some scientists say that up to 30 house-sized chunks of ice are hitting our planet's atmosphere every minute. Each of these big snowballs weighs about 20 tons. We're not up to our noses in snow because the ice melts while still thousands of miles above Earth.

▶ BIG LIGHT
The Pistol Star cannot be seen without a telescope, yet it sends out 10 million times more energy than our Sun! Newly discovered, it is believed to be 186 million to 280 million miles across—about as big as Earth's orbit around the Sun.

ANOTHER COMPANION
Earth travels with more than just a moon—Asteroid 3753, just over three miles in diameter, is trapped by Earth's gravity into a strange orbit between Mercury and Mars. It takes 770 years for this asteroid to orbit Earth.

◀ HOT BLOB
When electrically charged gas gets ejected from the Sun, a blob of it may weigh tens of billions of tons, travel about 2.2 million miles per hour, and carry enough energy to boil off the Mediterranean Sea. When it hits Earth's atmosphere, a geomagnetic storm occurs, sending curtains of colorful light called auroras over the polar skies.

◀ HOME UNKNOWN
What is the best-mapped planet in our solar system? Not Earth! More than 98 percent of Venus's surface has been mapped, thanks to the explorer spacecraft *Magellan*. Here on Earth, more than two-thirds of the surface is covered with water, and much of it cannot be charted as accurately as the Venusian surface.

EERIE EARTH

Our home planet harbors a store of weird happenings, from powerful earthquakes to mysterious, phenomenal events. In 1811, things were rocking in New Madrid, Missouri. The area experienced the strongest earthquakes in recorded American history. More than 3,000 square miles of land were visibly damaged and, for a brief time, the Mississippi River flowed backwards!

SPIN CITY

The Moon's gravitation acts like a brake on Earth, slowing down its rotation. Each year our days get about 20 millionths of a second longer. But something else is having the reverse effect. Scientists have discovered that dams, in concentrating water away from the equator, are making the planet spin faster!

COMPASS CHECK ▲

The motion of molten metal in Earth's outer core produces an electric current, causing the planet to behave like a giant magnet. Earth's magnetic field extends about 37,000 miles into space and protects us from some of the Sun's most harmful particles. Curiously, the magnetic field reverses from time to time— the last occasion was about 700,000 years ago.

HIDDEN LAKE

A freshwater lake about the size of the state of New Jersey lies under more than two miles of ice in eastern Antarctica. The lake may be a mile deep in places. Bacteria and other life forms in Lake Vostok haven't been in contact with the surface for at least 50,000 years, and perhaps as long as three million years.

200 Million Years Ago

100 Million Years Ago

Today

▲ON THE MOVE

Think you can stand perfectly still? Guess again. Not only is Earth rocketing around the Sun at 66,600 miles per hour; it's spinning on its axis at about 1,000 miles per hour. Even the ground beneath you is never motionless, as big slabs of Earth's crust, called tectonic plates, are moving very slowly.

◀ Scientists believe that the continents were once all joined together, and that the movement of Earth's crust caused them to break apart. The Americas continue to drift away from Europe and Africa at a rate of one inch per year.

BIG BANG

When the Indonesian volcanic island of Krakatau blew itself to bits in 1883, a sound like distant cannons reached places nearly 3,000 miles away! The blast caused huge waves, called tsunamis (sue-NAH-mees), as far away as South America and shot ash an estimated 50 miles into the air.

PINGO PONG

In Siberia and northern Canada, frost stays in the ground year round, reaching as deep as 1,650 feet. Houses have to be built on stilts so they don't melt the frost and sink into the mud. Sometimes the frost pushes up piles of earth as high as 230 feet to create mounds called pingos.

DREAMS TO DEVICES

Scientists have built some weird and amazing things. Researchers in California have created the most powerful magnet in the world, 250,000 times as strong as Earth's magnetic field. Other scientists have created a light brighter than every star in our galaxy, concentrated in a spot the size of a pinhead. Called the Vulcan laser, it may enable scientists to look into living cells and capture molecules in action.

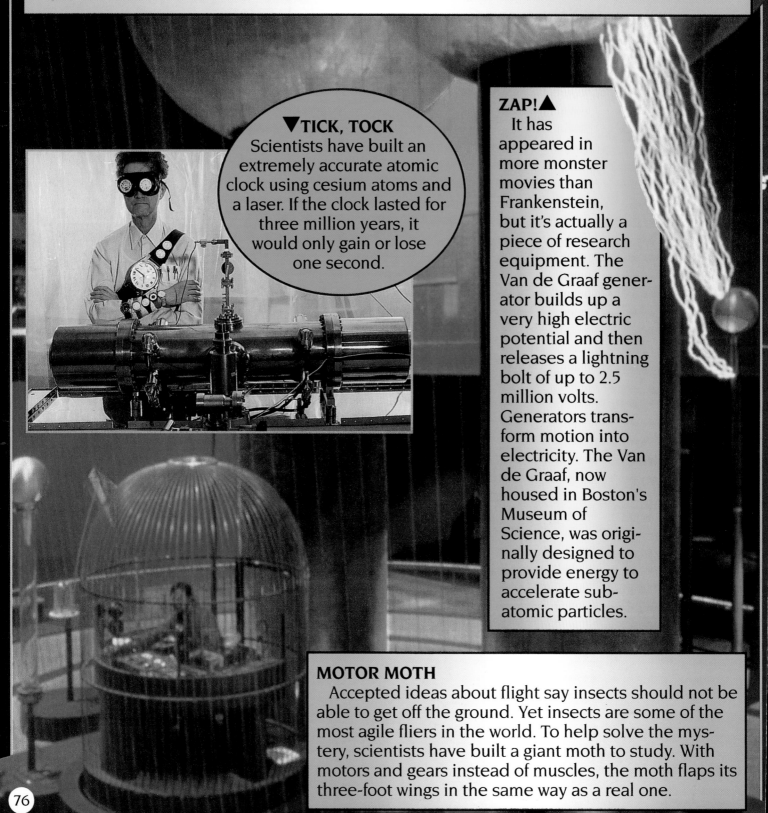

▼TICK, TOCK
Scientists have built an extremely accurate atomic clock using cesium atoms and a laser. If the clock lasted for three million years, it would only gain or lose one second.

ZAP!▲
It has appeared in more monster movies than Frankenstein, but it's actually a piece of research equipment. The Van de Graaf generator builds up a very high electric potential and then releases a lightning bolt of up to 2.5 million volts. Generators transform motion into electricity. The Van de Graaf, now housed in Boston's Museum of Science, was originally designed to provide energy to accelerate subatomic particles.

MOTOR MOTH
Accepted ideas about flight say insects should not be able to get off the ground. Yet insects are some of the most agile fliers in the world. To help solve the mystery, scientists have built a giant moth to study. With motors and gears instead of muscles, the moth flaps its three-foot wings in the same way as a real one.

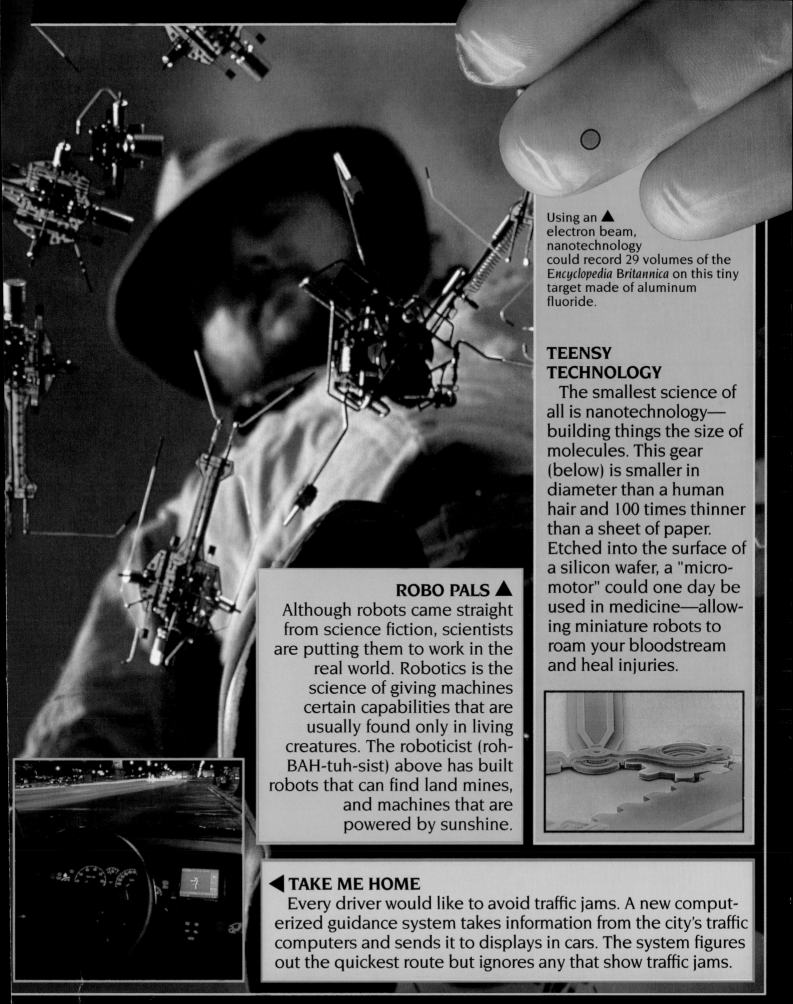

Using an ▲ electron beam, nanotechnology could record 29 volumes of the *Encyclopedia Britannica* on this tiny target made of aluminum fluoride.

TEENSY TECHNOLOGY

The smallest science of all is nanotechnology—building things the size of molecules. This gear (below) is smaller in diameter than a human hair and 100 times thinner than a sheet of paper. Etched into the surface of a silicon wafer, a "micro-motor" could one day be used in medicine—allowing miniature robots to roam your bloodstream and heal injuries.

ROBO PALS ▲

Although robots came straight from science fiction, scientists are putting them to work in the real world. Robotics is the science of giving machines certain capabilities that are usually found only in living creatures. The roboticist (roh-BAH-tuh-sist) above has built robots that can find land mines, and machines that are powered by sunshine.

◀ TAKE ME HOME

Every driver would like to avoid traffic jams. A new comput-erized guidance system takes information from the city's traffic computers and sends it to displays in cars. The system figures out the quickest route but ignores any that show traffic jams.

STRANGE STUFF

Sometimes when we think of science, images of smoking beakers come to mind. In the laboratory, scientists can discover or create some pretty weird things.

▼ Solid carbon dioxide, known as dry ice, becomes a gas when mixed with water, producing thick clouds of fog.

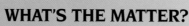

◀ BUCKYBALLS?

Sixty carbon atoms arranged in a perfect sphere make up a molecule of buck-minsterfullerene, or a "buckyball." Because of their shape, these molecules have been named after Buckminster Fuller, an engineer who developed the domed stadium. Buckyballs can be found in the soot floating around after you blow out a candle. Other such hollow carbon molecules are called bunny balls, bucky-babies, and bucky onions.

WHAT'S THE MATTER?

Solid, liquid, gas, plasma—the four states of matter. Now there's a weird fifth form—clusters. Clusters are groups of atoms that seem to be some-where between atoms and the regular-sized world. They have strange electrical, optical, and magnetic properties.

STRETCHED THICK

If you punch a pillow, your fist leaves a dent in the surface. But some strange substances called auxetic (og-ZED-ik) mate-rials don't act this way. When stretched, they get thicker. A pillow made of auxetic material would expand when punched.

◀ LIGHTWEIGHT

Scientists have made silica, the raw material for glass, into something new—an aerogel (AIR-oh-jell). The substance con-tains as much as 96 percent air and weighs far less than glass. Because it's so clear, aerogel is hard to find once it is placed on a lab bench. Here, it is shown supporting a weight and a penny.

GENIE IN A BOTTLE?

No, it's not magic. It's a hologram, a photograph taken with laser light. One set of light waves is sent to the object, which reflects the light onto film. Another set of light waves, sent directly to the film, intersects the reflected light waves and creates a 3-D image. You can walk all the way around the picture to view it from different angles.

VIRTUAL LAB

Sometimes it's difficult, or completely impossible, for scientists to conduct their studies in real-life places. Virtual reality, simulated by computers, takes them there—or appears to.

◀ In a virtual molecular interaction, a researcher can pick up molecules, reorient them, and study what occurs.

EARTH'S TREASURES

We spend most of our time above ground, walking on Earth's crust. Now it's time to take a look beneath the surface. There we'll find sparkling gems, deep caves, subterranean lakes and rivers, and more. Grab your shovel, and let's uncover the secrets hidden beneath our feet!

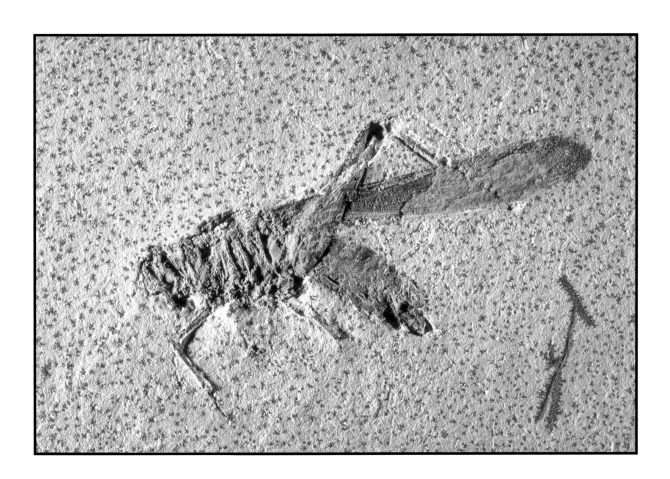

PLANET EARTH

From his moon-bound spaceship, the astronaut Neil Armstrong described Planet Earth as "a beautiful jewel in space." This beautiful jewel on which we live is about 4.6 billion years old, has a diameter of 7,926 miles, and measures 24,901 miles around at the equator, its thickest part.

HARD ROCK

If you look at pictures taken from space, you may think of the Earth as a planet covered mostly by water. It's true that water is one of Earth's unique characteristics compared to other planets. But have you ever wondered what's below the oceans and the soil of the continents? A crust of hard rock, ranging from 4 to 44 miles thick.

HOT, HOT, HOT

The Earth is made up of four layers that get hotter the deeper they go. Under the crust is the mantle, which is solid rock topped with molten, or liquid, rock called magma. Beneath the mantle is a layer of fiery liquid metals, called the outer core. The inner core is a solid ball of nickel and iron, estimated to be over 7,000°F.

Crust

Mantle

Outer Core

Inner Core

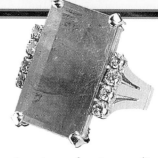

Snowflake obsidian

A watermelon tourmaline gem set with diamonds.

NATURAL TREASURES

Rich in natural resources, Earth is a treasure box of rocks, minerals, gems, and crystals. These materials are formed by processes above and below the surface of the Earth.

The mineral variscite.

Amethyst crystals

SMOOTH MOVE

Though you can't feel it, except during an earthquake, the crust of the Earth is constantly changing. That's because the crust is not solid but is made up of *tectonic* plates that move. During this movement, the rocky crust gets pushed up, causing mountains to form or grow.

▲ Earth's highest mountain range, the Himalayas, were formed about 45 million years ago when two tectonic plates collided and the seafloor between them buckled up.

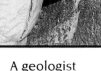

A geologist at work.

◀ ROCK HOUNDS

Geologists are people who study the Earth's rocky crust. Rocks, for them, are like pages from a living history book, providing information on how the Earth was formed. Scientists who study how, when, and why rocks were formed are called petrologists. Scientists who study minerals are known as mineralogists.

ERUPTION!

Volcanic mountains are made when one plate sinks beneath the other and red-hot magma is forced up through cracks in the Earth's surface. In this fiery liquid you can imagine the extreme temperatures and forces below the crust. Volcanic action is one force responsible for the formation of rocks and minerals.

A lava fountain in Hawaii.

83

THE BIRTH OF ROCKS AND MINERALS

Our planet is rich with life—millions of animals and thousands of plants. But there is also a wealth of nonliving things. Rocks and minerals are *inorganic*—not usually formed by plants or animals. There are over 3,600 minerals and more than a hundred types of rocks, made naturally by the Earth.

▶ Rocks are made from one or more kinds of minerals. The Dolomite Alps, in Italy, are made of a rock that consists of only one mineral—dolomite.

▲ Salt workers in Thailand.

FOOD FOR THOUGHT

Minerals may not be organic, but there are some minerals that you eat. You shake out one kind over your food. That's right! Common table salt, a valuable resource, is a mineral, and it's mined.

▼ IT'S A HARD ROCK LIFE

Rocks have a life cycle. They change and transform. From molten material, sometimes spewed from volcanoes, *igneous rocks* are formed. Worn down by the forces of erosion—wind, rain, frost, and ice—these rocks break up into smaller and smaller pieces, called *sediments*, which are deposited in rivers or the ocean. As layers of sediment build up, they form new, *sedimentary rocks*. Rocks can also be transformed by heat and pressure inside the Earth and become *metamorphic rocks*.

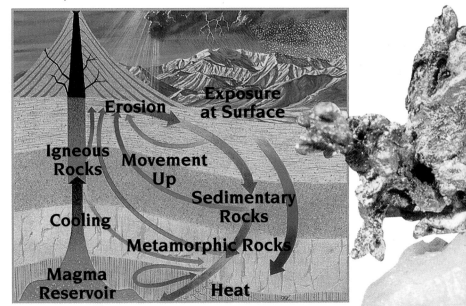

Erosion
Exposure at Surface
Igneous Rocks
Movement Up
Sedimentary Rocks
Cooling
Metamorphic Rocks
Magma Reservoir
Heat

▼ JUST FOR DECORATION

Certain rocks and minerals make beautiful decorative objects. Rocks are tumbled and polished. Minerals are cut into gemstones for jewelry. One very popular mineral is agate. Found in volcanic rocks, these stripy stones are often sliced, dyed, polished and displayed.

MINERAL CREATION

You've heard that gold is found in "veins." But minerals are not just formed in the cracks of rocks. They come from the fires of volcanoes, crystallize in granite rocks, solidify out of evaporating water, and arise from severe forces of heat and pressure within the Earth.

Gypsum roses

FANTASTIC FORMS

Minerals form some incredible shapes. They may start out dissolved in air or in water, but over time, heat and pressure turn them into solid matter with a crystalline structure. This process is called *crystallization*. With desert rose, leaflike crystals form when ground water in the desert evaporates, and the minerals gypsum and barite crystallize.

Barite roses

MICRO ART ▼

Maybe you don't think of science as a colorful business. Well, think again! This lovely picture is a photomicrograph (foe-tuh-MIE-cruh-graf). It was taken after slicing a specimen and viewing it under a high-powered microscope. The picture reveals much about the crystals that lie within.

VOLCANIC ACTION

An erupting volcano is a spectacular and frightening sight. When red-hot liquid magma finds a weak spot in the Earth's crust, it comes spewing out above the surface, hurling lava, ash, and rocks called volcanic bombs.

In 1980, Mt. St. Helen's, a volcanic mountain in the state of Washington, literally blew its top.

LAVA ▼

The fiery magma that rushes out the throat or escapes through side vents in a volcano is called lava. If thick and sticky, it can build up a cone-shaped mountain as it quickly cools and solidifies on the Earth's surface. If thin and runny, the lava flows farther, at speeds of more than 360 miles per hour. It cools and hardens more slowly, creating lower mounds called shield volcanoes.

▲ RING OF FIRE

Most volcanoes are found where the Earth's crust is thinnest, at the edges of tectonic plates or in the middle of oceans. In an area around the Pacific Ocean known as the Ring of Fire, there is a great deal of volcanic activity.

EXTRUSIVE ROCKS

Rocks formed from lava are called *igneous*, which means fiery. If the lava quickly cools and hardens on the Earth's surface, the rocks are said to be *extrusive*.

NATURAL GLASS ▶

Obsidian, a natural glass, is a shiny black extrusive rock. Because it breaks easily into sharp-edged pieces, early humans used it to make hunting tools.

◀ COOL COLUMNS

Basalt is the most common extrusive rock. When basaltic lava cools, it sometimes splits into columns, like these at Giant's Causeway in Northern Ireland.

INTRUSIVE ROCKS

Igneous rocks that solidify inside the Earth's crust are called *intrusive*. They contain crystallized minerals that give the rocks a granular texture and color.

▼ Scientists called *volcanologists* cross the ropy surface of hard lava to learn more about the mysteries within our Earth.

GRAVESTONE

The most common intrusive rock of the Earth's outermost crust, granite is found in many parts of the world. This stone varies in color according to the minerals it contains. A hard and heavy stone, slabs of granite are used to cover buildings, pave walkways, or make gravestones.

Granite

Serpentine

THE PHARAOH'S GIFT

Serpentine is a fine-grained intrusive rock. This stone was quite valuable to ancient Egyptians. Like alabaster and other soft stones used for carving, serpentine belonged to the pharaoh, or king. No one could use these materials unless the pharaoh gave the stones to them.

BREAKDOWN

How do you get sedimentary rocks? Erosion wears at the surface of rocks, and then wind and rain carry the sediments to new locations, often to the sea or to riverbeds. Over millions of years, layers of sediment become buried, one on top of the next. The weight of the upper layer presses down on the lower layers and cements them together into sedimentary rocks.

◀ One of the world's greatest natural wonders, the Grand Canyon in Arizona, was formed by the erosion of two different sedimentary rocks—red sandstone and limestone.

MIRACLE MUD ▼

You may call it mud, but clay is a sediment full of minerals. Found near water, often in the banks of streams and rivers, clay may be gray, black, white, or yellowish. When it's wet, it feels sticky. But when it's packed together, the water gets forced out and clay eventually forms hard rocks called mudstone or shale.

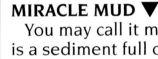

SANDSTONE ▲

Sandstone is a gritty rock composed of layers of sand grains that are firmly pressed together. Because sandstone is fairly soft, it is easily carved. Native Americans in the Southwest carved dwellings out of sandstone cliffs.

▲ PUDDING STONES

Conglomerate rocks are sometimes called pudding stones, but you wouldn't want to sink your teeth into one! A conglomerate is formed when various rocks and pebbles are buried and become cemented together. Pudding stones are often found at the seashore or in riverbeds.

CAVE CARVING

Dark, eerie caverns and tunnels are hidden beneath limestone mountains. That's because limestone, a sedimentary rock, is *porous*—meaning it's full of tiny holes and cracks that allow water to pass through. Over thousands of years, weakly acidic water dripping through makes the cracks wider and carves out caves and tunnels in the soft limestone.

Carlsbad Caverns in Arizona. ▶

▼ EARTHENWARE

Artisans began shaping clay into eating vessels, storage containers, and art objects thousands of years ago. When fired, or dried out, clay becomes hard and its surface can be painted.

SPELUNK IT!

Entering a cave is a fascinating adventure. A cave is full of weird rocks called *stalactites*, which hang from the ceiling and walls, and *stalagmites*, which form on the floor. Scientists who study caves are called speleologists. Other people who explore caves are called spelunkers.

◀ These two spelunkers are exploring the biggest cave system in the world—Mammoth Caves in Kentucky, which run 347 miles underground.

FOSSIL FIND

Did you know that most fossils are found in sedimentary rocks, such as limestone? The reason is simple. When the body of a dead plant or animal gets covered by sediment, that sediment slowly turns to stone. What remains of the plant or animal also becomes stone, or a fossil.

▲ This limestone shows the presence of marine fossils. Egyptians carved limestone into coffins called sarcophagi (sar-KA-fuh-gie), a word that literally means "flesh-eating stone."

Schist, full of recrystallized minerals, comes from shale or mud that has been cooked within the Earth.

ROCK CHANGE

Transformation. That is the secret to *metamorphic* rocks, which are igneous or sedimentary rocks that are pushed back into the Earth and changed by underground heat, or pressure, or both. During mountain-building processes, buried rocks are squeezed, folded, and heated up. The minerals within them then recrystallize and form new minerals.

▼ CAST OF COLORS

Prized for its many rich colors and textures, marble is one of the most beautiful rocks on Earth. Pure marble is white, but different minerals can turn it green, red, yellow, or black. When polished, marble takes on a glossy sheen.

◀ WRITING ON THE WALL

Rock isn't used just for building. It's also used for communication. Or it used to be. *Petroglyphs* are a form of writing. They're made by inscribing pictures on rock. At Newspaper Rock State Park in Utah, you can see such ancient communications.

▼ MAGIC MARBLE

What's a good example of metamorphic magic? Marble! This stone, found in mountainous regions throughout the world, is created when sedimentary limestone is exposed to high heat and new crystals of calcite grow within.

BUILDING BEAUTY

Centuries ago, people used solid marble to construct magnificent temples, palaces, and monuments. Later, they used pieces of cut, polished marble to add richness to the walls and floors of important buildings.

Built in 447 B.C. as a temple to the ▶ goddess Athena, the Parthenon in Athens, Greece, is made of solid marble.

▲ Slate is so abundant in Wales that the Welsh use it to shingle the roofs of their houses.

▲ The sedimentary stone known as shale.

SHALE SQUEEZE

Slate is formed during mountain building, when shale is squeezed so hard that the flaky mineral mica recrystallizes within it. The resulting rock is dark gray and splits easily into thin sheets.

COLLECTING CARRARA

A quarry is a place where slabs of stone are cut out of the sides of mountains. The stone is blasted out or cut with special saws. After it's quarried, marble is shipped around the world. Carrara, the most famous marble in the world, comes from a quarry in Tuscany, Italy.

SOFT STONE

Believe it or not, marble is a "soft" stone. That's why it's used in sculpting. Artists use a chisel and a hammer to chip and carve the stone into the shape they want, then polish it. The 16th-century Italian artist named Michelangelo used marble to sculpt many of his famous works.

An artist polishing a marble sculpture.

LIVING WITH MINERALS

People have used minerals even since prehistoric times. Today, industries depend on them to make products like paper, glass, and chemicals. Minerals are all around you, and they're all very different—in hardness, color, and luster. But there are ways to identify them.

◀ As beautiful as it is, sulfur's smell is not so attractive. It's used to make insecticides.

NOT SO HARD

Hardness is not so hard to test, thanks to Frederick Mohs, a German mineralogist who devised a scratch test in 1822. Mohs selected 10 minerals and assigned them numbers for increasing hardness. By scratching these known minerals with an unknown specimen, you can determine the specimen's relative hardness. The softer mineral will always show the scratch. You can also use some household items to test your specimen.

MOHS'S SCALE	HOUSEHOLD TEST
1. Talc	Scratch with fingernail
2. Gypsum	Scratch with fingernail
3. Calcite	Scratch with penny
4. Fluorite	Scratch with knife
5. Apatite	Scratch with knife
6. Orthoclase	Scratches glass
7. Quartz	Scratches glass
8. Topaz	Scratches glass
9. Corundum	Scratches glass
10. Diamond	Scratches glass

RUBIES ARE RED

Every mineral has certain characteristics that act as clues to help identify it. Color is one clue. If it's red, it might be a ruby, because rubies are always red.

MAGNETIC MINERAL

Ever feel drawn to certain minerals? Metals certainly do, because certain minerals, such as magnetite, are magnetic. Early explorers like Christopher Columbus used compasses made from magnetite when navigating.

▲ Orthoclase has a pearly luster.

LUSTER

The surface of a mineral reflects light. Mineral reflections, called *luster*, or sheen, include dull, glassy, metallic, or pearly.

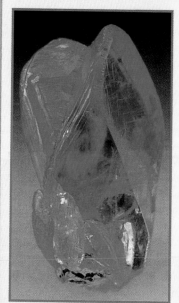

◀ It's not glass, but this mineral has a glassy luster.

SPLIT UP

The way a mineral splits when broken may help identify it. This property is called *cleavage*. Galena (at right) is said to have good cleavage.
Minerals that have little or no cleavage are said to have fracture. They sometimes crumble.

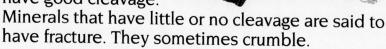

◀ Look into this calcite and you'll see double, because calcite's structure splits light into two rays instead of one.

SEE THROUGH

You can see right through some minerals, and they are called *transparent*. But if you can't see through a mineral clearly, it's *translucent*, letting through only some light. O*paque* minerals are the ones you can't see through at all.

◀ This primitive artwork is one of about 300 paintings from a cave discovered in southern France in 1994.

PRIMITIVE PAINT

The first paints ever used were minerals. Primitive artists who decorated the walls of caves ground up minerals from rocks for color. Early Native Americans crushed hematite into a powder, then mixed it with water to create the reddish-brown paint used to decorate their bodies.

METALLIC WORLD

It's a metallic world. Look around and you'll see the flashy sheen of metallic cars, airplanes, tools, machines, bridges, soda cans, pots and pans. Where does it all come from? Usually, metals are mined from rocks in the Earth's crust. But the process doesn't stop there. These materials need a lot of work to be useful.

MINING ▲

Many ore minerals are first discovered above ground, but then deep shafts and tunnels are dug so that more ore can be extracted. Miners go deep down into the Earth, day after day, to dig out valuable rocks. It's hard and sometimes dangerous work.

Gold is melted and poured into molds to make bars.

ORE STORE

Most useful metals are mined as ore. An ore is a rock that contains a metal, such as copper or gold. Once they're mined, ores must be crushed, separated, and refined.

▲ GOLD BARS ▲

It takes two tons of rock to extract just one ounce of gold. But that one ounce of metal is worth a lot of money. Valued for its beauty and rarity, gold has long been made into precious jewelry and used as a form of currency. People no longer buy things with gold coins, but gold is still made into bars and buried in bank vaults for investment purposes.

PAN IT!

Sometimes grains of gold break free from eroded rocks. The gold may get washed with other sediments down to a river or stream, where fortune hunters swirl the sediments in a water-filled pan to separate gold nuggets from the gravel.

These young panners are searching for gold nuggets.

◀ GOING PLATINUM

Durable, weighty, and glowing with a radiant luster, platinum is more valuable than gold. Although it is put to some very glamorous uses in jewelry, platinum is also used as dental fillings and to reduce pollution from car exhausts.

PICTURE THIS

In ancient Rome, silver was the more prized of metals. Today it's still valuable, especially where photography is concerned. Unlike gold or platinum, silver tarnishes, or discolors, when exposed to air. Light-sensitive silver salts are, therefore, used to coat camera film. Every time you take a picture you're tarnishing silver.

Silver is still used in jewelry, especially by renowned Navajo silversmiths.

Silver flatware is polished to remove the tarnish.

A bronze statue of Marcus Aurelius, a Roman emperor and philosopher.

MIXING METALS

The Bronze Age marked an important technological advance for humankind. Around 3000 B.C., it was discovered that adding tin to copper would create a harder metal, called bronze. Such a metal, formed when two or more metals are melted together, is called an alloy. Today, steel is the strongest alloy around. A product of modern times, steel is the skeleton of skyscrapers.

95

CRYSTAL CLEAR

Crystals are everywhere on Earth. They are diamonds, which can be cut into sparkling gems. They are also the grains of sand on a beach.

▲ A diamond rough and two cut stones.

◀ **SUPER SEVEN**
Growing is what crystals do, and they do it in an orderly fashion. Although there are thousands of crystal shapes in the world, they all fall into seven categories (classes) based on the symmetry, or form, of the crystal.

Cubic-shaped cuprite belongs to the cubic crystal system.

◀ TWO MAKES TWINS

Crystals don't always grow alone. Sometimes two of the same mineral will grow together, forming twinned crystals that look like butterfly wings. Or the two parts can grow into each other, forming a penetration twin, such as a fairy cross (at left).

SPINY HABIT ▶

It may look like a piece of a pine tree, but it's really a crystal known as cuprosklodowskite (COO-pro-skloe-dow-skite). The general shape a crystal takes is called its habit.

With cuprosklodowskite, the habit is needlelike. The needles are fragile, but they're sharp enough to puncture skin.

◀ Sulfur is *idiochromatic*, meaning it's nearly always the same color—bright yellow!

BLAZING ▶ COLOR

A crystal can dazzle the eye with its brilliant color. Depending on the impurities present, crystals of a particular mineral can be different colors. Quartz crystals look like glass when they're pure. When an iron impurity is present, you may get citrine, a golden variety of quartz.

▲ ON THE BALL

As far as we know, the ancient Greeks and Romans were the first to claim they could see the future by gazing into a polished crystal ball. Even today, fortune-tellers make the claim. Whether it is a window to the future or not, the beauty of such a perfect sphere of pure quartz may mesmerize even the nonbeliever.

TECHNO-CRYSTALS

Crystals really come in handy. Scientists have discovered that crystals do some pretty amazing things. They've also learned how to grow synthetic, or artificial, crystals in the laboratory. Synthetic crystals such as silicon are an important part of modern technology, used extensively in computers and other electronics.

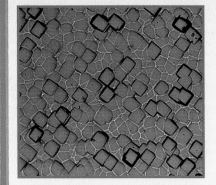

▲ A silicon chip.

GOOD VIBRATIONS

Over a hundred years ago, it was discovered that certain crystals vibrate when they come in contact with an electrical charge. Quartz vibrates more than 30,000 times per second. The pulse is so regular, quartz crystals can be used in watches to tick off time. In fact, there's such a demand for them, they're now made in laboratories.

◀ Quartz

A laboratory-grown ruby.

MAKE YOUR OWN

Once scientists discovered how diamond crystals form, they learned how to grow them in the lab. Today, scientists use a variety of techniques to grow flawless diamonds, rubies, and emeralds.

THE PRESSURE'S ON

Do you know of a crystal valued by the U.S. Navy? Tourmaline is definitely one. It takes on an electrical charge when heated or subjected to changes in pressure. For this reason, the crystal is used in pressure-detecting gauges in submarines.

LASER CUT ▶

Light directed through certain synthetic crystals, such as rubies, becomes a sharp laser beam. A laser can be focused to such a precise spot, its heat cuts through solid matter.

Doctors now use lasers instead of scalpels in some surgical operations.

This diamond is industrial grade.

OUT IN SPACE

Crystals of diamond can withstand even the extreme conditions of outer space. A diamond window in the Pioneer Venus probe allowed pictures to be taken in the scorching atmosphere of Venus.

LAY IT ON ▲

Throughout history, people have believed certain crystals have the power to heal or protect. Today's New Age healers say that crystals placed on the body will increase energy and healing. Crystal healing is sometimes referred to as "the laying on of stones."

CRYSTAL LAB

Growing crystals is something you can do at home. With the help of an adult, you can turn your kitchen into a crystal laboratory. You'll need the following:

1. A jar or plastic cup
2. 3 tablespoons of water
3. 3 tablespoons of liquid laundry bluing
4. 3 tablespoons of salt
5. 1 tablespoon of ammonia
6. A second container, such as a margarine tub or an aluminum pie pan
7. Assorted rocks and a broken piece of charcoal briquette

Mix the water, bluing, salt, and ammonia together in the jar or cup. Then, in the pie pan, arrange the rocks and charcoal briquette. Spoon the solution over the rocks and charcoal. Let it sit undisturbed for at least 24 hours.

You'll be surprised at what you've created.

WHAT A GEM!

When you think of treasure, you may think of gems—diamonds, rubies, sapphires, and even garnets. Gemstones are minerals with great ornamental value. That value is determined by their clarity, transparency, color, brilliance, fire (dispersion), and hardness. Beauty and rarity also have something to do with the value of a gem, but beauty, of course, is in the eye of the beholder.

A collection of differently colored garnets.

THE HOPE

Diamonds aren't always clear and colorless. They may be black, pink, yellow . . . or blue, like the famous Hope Diamond. The Hope is 44.52 carats worth of stone, and has been valued at $200,000,000.

UNCONQUERABLE

Diamonds are probably the best-known gems in the world, valued for their fire and supreme hardness. The word "diamond" actually comes from the Greek word "adamas," which means "unconquerable."

DIAMOND FIND

The huge diamond known as the Star of Africa was cut from the largest diamond ever found, the Cullinan crystal, which weighed 3,106 carats. A carat is one-fifth of a gram, or .035 ounces. So, the Cullinan weighed in at one and a half pounds. It was eventually cut into 105 different stones. Two of the largest Cullinan stones now rest in the British imperial state crown.

▲ COLOR FLASH

Although it's important for a gem to be hard enough to be worn every day, some are actually quite fragile. Opal has a tendency to crack and chip, but its flashes of color make it a popular gemstone.

100

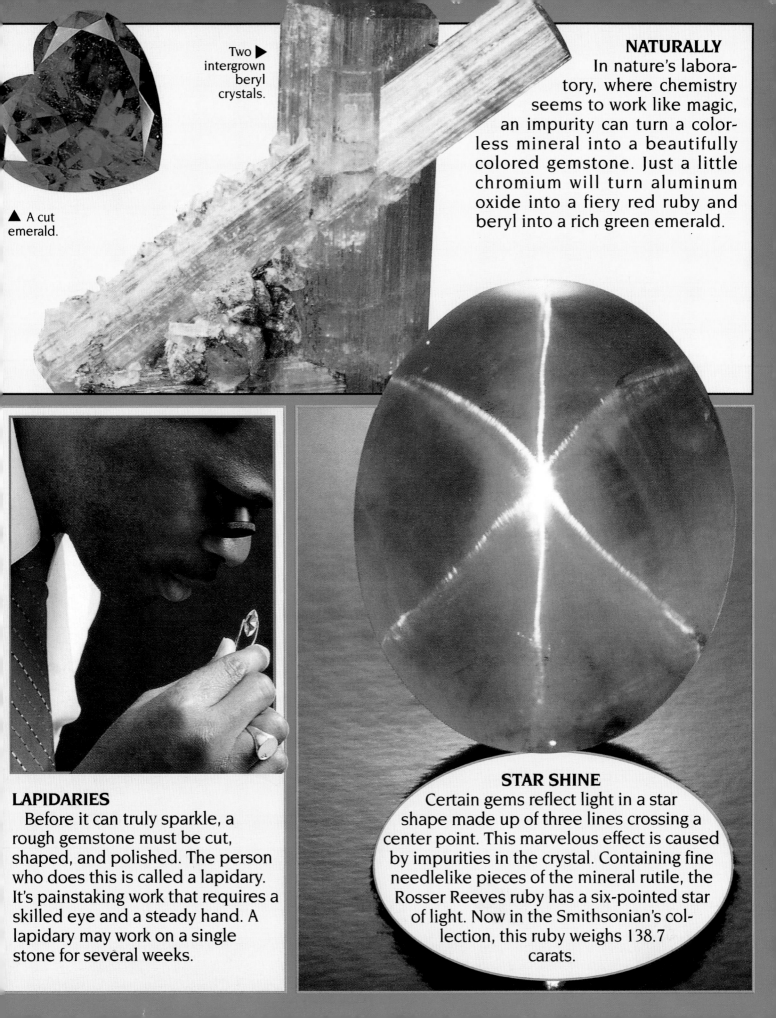

▲ A cut emerald.

Two ► intergrown beryl crystals.

NATURALLY

In nature's laboratory, where chemistry seems to work like magic, an impurity can turn a colorless mineral into a beautifully colored gemstone. Just a little chromium will turn aluminum oxide into a fiery red ruby and beryl into a rich green emerald.

LAPIDARIES

Before it can truly sparkle, a rough gemstone must be cut, shaped, and polished. The person who does this is called a lapidary. It's painstaking work that requires a skilled eye and a steady hand. A lapidary may work on a single stone for several weeks.

STAR SHINE

Certain gems reflect light in a star shape made up of three lines crossing a center point. This marvelous effect is caused by impurities in the crystal. Containing fine needlelike pieces of the mineral rutile, the Rosser Reeves ruby has a six-pointed star of light. Now in the Smithsonian's collection, this ruby weighs 138.7 carats.

GEMS-A-PLENTY

We tend to think of gems as rare objects. Maybe it's their amazing sparkle or bold colors, combined with the fact that they're made by nature. But gems are all around us, very much a part of our lives and our cultures. Even since prehistoric times, people have sought out objects to ornament their bodies or their homes.

◀ In this perfume bottle, you can see citrine, jade, sapphire, amethyst, and gold.

▲ Petrified wood is a fossil that has long been used to make jewelry.

FOSSIL GEM

Organic gems are derived from once-living plants and animals. The gem known as amber is formed from the sticky sap secreted by pine trees 50 million years ago. Sometimes the ancient body of an insect or other small animal is trapped inside. Used since prehistoric times for jewelry, amber is still a popular gemstone.

▼ A piece of amber with a fossilized insect.

JADE ▶

The ancient Chinese sometimes buried their dead in suits of jade. They believed that this hard gemstone had magical powers and would preserve the dead person's spirit. Jadeite and nephrite are two different minerals, but the opaque gemstones they form are both called jade. We think of jade as green, but it can be many colors.

A Chinese carving of jadeite.

◀ TURQUOISE

This stone has been used since ancient times. The Egyptians ornamented mummies with turquoise. Native Americans in the southwestern United States have been carving the opaque blue-green stone into jewelry for thousands of years.

▲ Turquoise in the rough.

◀ BORN OF SAND ▶

Pearls are organic gems that grow when a grain of sand lodges inside an oyster or mussel shell, and the animal surrounds it with a shiny white substance called *nacre*. Pearl divers still scour the deep for these underwater gems, especially in the Persian Gulf and the seas around Malaysia and Australia.

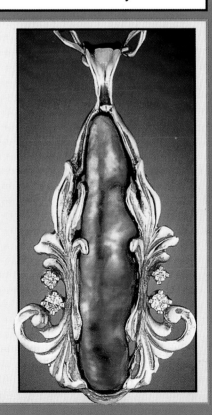

A free-form pearl formed by an Abalone mollusk.

BIRTHSTONES

January Garnet

February Amethyst

BIRTHDAY LUCK

There are special gemstones, called *birthstones*, which represent each month in the year. Nobody knows how, why, or where the custom started, but many people believe that wearing their birthstone will bring them good luck.

March Aquamarine

April Diamond

May Emerald

June Pearl

July Ruby

August Sardonyx

September Sapphire

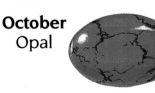

October Opal

November Topaz

December Turquoise

TREASURE HUNT

The treasures of the Earth are all around you, just waiting to be discovered. If you want to collect them, look around where you live. You may find black, white, and other colored crystals in gravel or sand. Also, contact a local mineral society. They sometimes schedule field trips to nearby areas where you can explore for specimens.

▲ DIRT DETECTIVES

Who knows? If you're an amateur rock hound today, tomorrow you may decide to become a petrologist, geologist, or mineralogist. Also, there are some scientists who combine police work with their study of rocks and minerals. Working for the FBI, these detectives analyze specimens found near crime scenes and try to match them with minerals in the soil found on suspected criminals or on "getaway" cars.

◄ You can get great crystals of pyrite from nature stores or find chunks of this mineral in Arizona and Colorado.

THUNDEREGGS ▲
Geodes, also called thundereggs, look like dull rocks on the outside, but when split open they reveal a sparkling inner surprise. These wonders form when fluids filtering through the rocks crystallize within. Geodes, found in hardened lava, are prized by crystal collectors. The one above is chock-full of amethyst.

FINDING FOSSILS
Fossils tell us about the creatures that lived on Earth millions of years ago. The creature may have been an enormous swamp-dwelling dinosaur, or a small fish or shell in a long-vanished ocean. Fossils of prehistoric teeth, bones, and shells, all found in limestone, are more common than you might expect.

◄ A great white's tooth (far left), and the fossil tooth of its ancestor—the megalodon.

GEM ISLAND ▶

Sri Lanka, an island in the Indian Ocean, is known as "Gem Island" because so many valuable gemstones are found there. During typhoons, the gems are washed down the sides of mountains along with rocks and mud. Gem hunters scoop up the thick mud and strain it through baskets in the hopes of finding valuable stones.

◀ CYBER ART ▲

What can you do with gems besides wear them or sit them on a shelf? With today's computer equipment, pictures of gems can be transformed into incredible science-fiction images. These cyber gems, with their fantastic colors and otherworldly formations, were created from photographs of crystals.

Glossary

acupuncture: medical procedure in which needles are inserted into certain points of the body

anthropologist: scientist who studies humankind

aquaculture: the breeding of fish in pens for humans to eat; similar to a farm

Aqua Lung: breathing device, consisting of air-filled tanks, that allows people to explore deep waters

aquanaut: scientist who spends a long period of time living and studying underwater

archaeologist: scientist who studies past cultures

asteroid: an object, such as a large rock, found in space

atoll: ring of coral that forms around a sunken volcano

auroras: colored lights in the sky, visible in the northern and southern polar regions

bathyscape: vehicle used to explore very deep parts of the ocean

cluster: fifth state of matter that has electrical, optical, and magnetic characteristics

dust devil: a swirl of dirt created when a tornado travels through a desert

earthquake: shaking of the ground caused by sudden shifts of rock beneath Earth's surface

equator: imaginary line dividing Earth into two equal parts

excavate: to dig or hollow out

food chain: series of living things in which each feeds upon the one below it and, in turn, is eaten by the one above it; the cycle repeats itself until the tiniest animal eats the bacteria that is left behind from the largest animal.

Fujita scale: scale used to describe the severity of tornadoes

gale: a strong wind blowing at speeds of more than 32 miles per hour

gravity: magnetic force that pulls objects toward the center of a large body, such as a planet

hurricane: violent storm with heavy rains and winds that reach speeds of at least 74 miles per hour

landslide: the quick, downward movement of land caused by an earthquake or excessive rain

magma: liquid rock

marine biologist: scientist who studies the oceans and the plants and animals that live there

meteorite: an object from space (usually made of rock or metal) that falls to Earth

mollusk: animal that has a soft body and no backbone, and may live in a shell. Snails, clams, and octopuses are mollusks

nanotechnology: the science of building tiny things that can be seen only with the use of high-powered instruments

orbit: path of a planet or other space body moving around another object, such as a star

paleontologist: a scientist who studies fossils

plague: a serious and contagious illness that affects many people in a short period of time

plasma: type of matter made up of high-temperature gases filled with positive and negative atomic particles

Richter scale: scale used to describe the severity of earthquakes

robotics: science of designing machines that can do complicated, often repetitive work

satellite: a natural or man-made object that orbits a larger body in space

sauropod: a four-legged, plant-eating dinosaur

school (of fish): a group that swims together

spawn: produce eggs

submersible: a small machine used for research that can withstand the great pressure and low temperatures of the very deep sea

tornado: violent, swirling storm often created by large thunderstorms

tsunami: giant wave caused by an underwater earthquake or volcanic eruption

volcano: an opening in Earth's crust out of which steam or magma can flow

Index

A

abalone, 17
acid rain, 30
acupuncture, 60
aerogel, 78
agate, 85
alabaster, 87
alloy, 95
Amazon River, 66
amber, 63, 102
America's Cup, 9
anchovies, 28
anemone, 19
anglerfish, 24
Antarctica, 26-27, 74
anthropologists, 70
Apatosaurus, 69
aquaculture, 31
Aqua Lung, 22
aquanauts, 23
archaeologists, 38, 70
Archimedes, 58
arctic, 26
Arctic Ocean, 8, 9
Argentinosaurus, 68
Argo, 23
Armenia, 41
Armstrong, Neil, 82
aspirin, 67
asteroids, 72, 73
Atlantic Ocean, 8, 26
    landscape of, 20
atoll, 19
atomic clock, 76
atoms, 59
    clusters, 78
auroras, 73
auxetic material, 78
avalanche, 49
Axel Heiberg Island, 68

B

bacteria, 11, 24, 58, 65, 74
bald eagles, 67
barite, 85
barnacles, 16
barrier reef, 19
basalt, 87
bathyscape, 22
bedbugs, 65
Beebe, Charles, 22
beluga whales, 26
biotechnology, 53
birthstones, 103
bivalves, 16
blizzards, 35, 48-49

blood cells, 64
bloodletting, 60
boats, 12-13
bogs, 71
brain coral, 19
bronze, 95
Bronze Age, 95
building and construction, 90
Burgess shale, 68

C

calcite, 90, 93
Carrara (marble), 91
carving rock, 88, 90
CAT scan, 71
cave paintings, 70, 93
caves, 89
Challenger, 24
Cheddar, England, 62
Chinese (ancient), 103
clams, 24
clay, 88, 89
Clean Water Act, 30
cleavage, 93
clownfish, 19
clusters, 78
coelacanth, 25
Columbus, Christopher, 13,
    71, 92
computers, 61, 70, 98
Cook, Captain James, 15
copper, 94, 95
coral polyps, 18
coral reef, 18-19
Cousteau, Jacques Yves, 22,
    31
crabs, 16, 17, 24, 66
cruise ship, 13
crystallization, 85, 87
crystals, 82, 85, 96-99, 104,
    105
    characteristics of, 96-97
    growing your own, 99
    healing, 99
    synthetic, 98-99
Cullinan crystal, 100
cures, 60-61
Curie, Marie, 61
cyclones, 44, 47

D-E-F

Del Cano, Juan Sebastian, 13
Democritus, 59
diamonds, 96, 98, 99, 100
dinosaurs, 68-69, 104
DNA, 62-63,

Dolly, 62
dolomite, 84
dolphins, 10, 31
dry ice, 78
Dust Bowl, 55
dust devil, 55
dust storm, 55
Earth, 8, 14, 58, 73, 74-75
    crust of, 20, 34, 43, 75,
    82-83
earthenware, 89
earthquakes, 34, 40-41, 42-43,
    74, 83
Egyptians (ancient), 87, 89,
    103
Einstein, Albert, 59
electricity and fish, 66
emeralds, 98, 101
equator, 9, 82
Ericson, Leif, 13
Eric the Red, 13
erosion, 84, 88
Eskimos, 27
Etna, Mt., 37
Exxon Valdez, 30
firefighters, 35
fish farm, 31
fishing, 28-29, 30
floods, 35, 52-53
food chain, 11
forest fires, 35, 50-51
fossils, 68-70, 89, 102, 104
fracture, 93
fringing reef, 19
Fujita scale, 45
Fujita, T. Theodore, 45
Fuller, R. Buckminster, 78

G-H-I

Gagnan, Emile, 22
gales, 55
Galileo, 58
Galveston, Texas, 47
gems and gemstones, 82, 85,
    100-103, 105
genetics, 61, 62-63
geodes, 104
geologists, 83, 104
germs, 58
Giant's Causeway, 87
Giganotosaurus, 68
Glenwood Springs, Colorado,
    50
gold, 85, 94, 95
gorgonian coral, 19
Grand Canyon, 88

gravity, 14, 74
Great Barrier Reef, 19
Great Dying, 69
Great Tri-State Tornado, 34
Greeks (ancient), 97
gulper fish, 24
habit (crystal form), 97
hail, 54
hatchetfish, 24
Herculaneum, 38, 39
hermit crab, 10
Heyerdahl, Thor, 15
hologram, 79
Hope Diamond, 100
horseshoe crab, 66
hunting tools (historic), 87
hurricanes, 35, 46-47
icefish, 26
Ice Man, 71
Indian Ocean, 8, 25, 47
Inuit, 27
iron, 82

J-K-L

jade, 103
Jefferson City, Missouri, 51
jewelry, 95, 102, 103
Johnson, Lyndon B., 50
Johnstown, Pennsylvania, 53
Kanto Plain, Japan, 41
kayak, 27
Kealakekua Bay, 15
kelp, 16
Kiluaea, Hawaii, 36
Kobe, Japan, 41
Koko, 67
Kon-Tiki, 15
Krakatau, Indonesia, 36, 75
landslides, 54
lapidaries, 101
lasers, 99
lava, 86-87
Leakey, Richard, 70
leeches, 60
lightning, 55
limestone, 88, 89, 90, 104
Los Angeles, California, 40
luster, 93

M

Magellan, 73
Magellan, Ferdinand, 13
maggots, 60
magma, 20, 36, 82-83, 86
magnets, 92
Malaysia, 103

Mammoth Caves (Kentucky), 89
manta ray, 10
marble, 90-91
Mariana Trench, 21, 23
marine biologist, 9, 23
matter, 78
meiofauna, 65
mermaids, 12
metals, 92, 94-95
Michelangelo, 91
microscopes, 64-65
Milky Way, 72
mineralogists, 83, 104
minerals, 82-84, 88, 90, 92-95
    characteristics of, 92-93
    creation of, 85
mining, 94
Mississippi River, 35, 74
mites, 65
Mohs, Frederick, 92
Mohs's Scale, 92
mollusks, 16, 28
moon, 14
moray eels, 19
mud, 88, 90, 105
mussels, 16
Muybridge, Eadweard, 59

N-O
nacre, 103
nanotechnology, 77
Native Americans, 88, 93, 95, 103
New Madrid, Missouri, 74
Newspaper Rock State Park (Utah), 90
Northern Hemisphere, 14
North Pole, 26
Northwest Passage, 26
Oakland, California, 50
oceans, 8-9, 14, 86
    drilling in, 28
    exploration of, 22-23
    inhabitants of, 10-11
    landscape of, 20-21
    pollution of, 30-31
    salt in, 8, 28
octopus, 10
opal, 100
opaque (minerals), 93
ore, 94

P
Pacific Ocean, 8, 21, 26, 42, 86
paint, 93
paleontologist, 68
Parthenon, 90
Pasteur, Louis, 58
pearl, 28, 103

pearl divers, 103
peat bog, 71
Peking Man, 70
Pelee, Mt., 37
penguins, 27-66
periwinkle snails, 16
Persian Gulf, 103
Peshtigo, Wisconsin, 51
petrified wood, 102
petroglyphs, 90
petrologists, 83, 104
photography, 95, 105
photomicrographs, 85
Piccard, Auguste, 23
Piccard, Jacques, 23
Pistol Star, 73
plankton, 10, 11, 18
platinum, 95
poison arrow frog, 61
pollen, 65
polyps, 18
Pompeii, Italy, 38, 39
prairie dogs, 67
Prince William Sound, Alaska, 41
pudding stones, 88

Q-R
quarry, 91
quartz crystals, 97, 98
queen conch shell, 16
Quetzalcoatlus, 69
radiation, 61
Red Sea, 8
Richter, Charles, 41
Richter scale, 40, 41
Ring of Fire, 21, 34, 41, 86
robotics, 77
rocks, 82-91, 94-95
    conglomerate, 88
    extrusive, 87
    igneous, 84, 87, 90
    intrusive, 87
    life cycle of, 84
    metamorphic, 84, 90
    sedimentary, 84, 88, 89, 90, 91
Romans (ancient), 97
Rome, Italy, 95
Rosser Reeves ruby, 101
rosy harp shell, 16
rubies, 92, 98, 99, 101

S
sailing, 9
St. Helens, Mt., 37, 49, 86
salmon, 11
salt, 84
San Andreas Fault, 43
sand, 96, 103

sandstone, 88
San Francisco, California, 42-43
sarcophagi (coffins), 89
satellites, 47
scallops, 16
scratch test (mineral hardness), 92
scuba diver, 18, 22
sea cucumber, 25
sea fans, 19
sea horses, 19
seajelly, 9
seals, 26, 27
sea otter, 17
seastars, 16
sea urchins, 16, 17
seaweed, 16, 17
sediments, 84, 89
seismograph, 41
shale, 88, 90, 91
sharks, 19, 31
Shasta Ski Bowl, Mt., 48
shellfish, 16, 19
shipwrecks, 22-23
Siebe, Augustus, 22
silicon, 98
silver, 95
slate, 91
Smokey the Bear, 50
snails, 16
sneezes, 65
snorkelers, 18
Southern Hemisphere, 14
South Pole, 26
space, 72-73
speleologists, 89
spelunkers, 89
sperm whale, 10
squid
    giant, 10
    monster, 12
Sri Lanka, 105
stalactites, 89
stalagmites, 89
Star of Africa, 100
Star II, 23
steel, 95
Stegosaurus, 69
submarines, 13, 98
submersibles, 13, 21, 23
sulfur, 92, 97
Sullivan, Roy, 55
Sumbawa, Indonesia, 36
surfing, 14, 15

T
Tangshan, China, 40
techno-crystals, 98-99
tectonic plates, 83, 86

thundereggs, 104
tide pools, 16
tides, 14, 46
tiger cowry shell, 16
Titanic, 23
Tornado Alley, 45
tornadoes, 34, 33-34, 44
tourmaline, 98
translucent (minerals), 93
transparent (minerals), 93
tsunamis, 15, 41
tube worms, 24
tuna, 28, 31
turquoise, 103
Tuscany, Italy, 91
typhoon, 47

V-W
Van de Graaf Generator, 76
Venus, 73, 99
Vesuvius, Mt., 38, 39
Vikings, 13, 71
viperfish, 24
Virgin Islands, 46
virtual reality, 79
viruses, 65
volcanoes, 20-21, 36-37, 83, 84, 85, 86-87
volcanologists, 37, 87
Vostok, Lake, 74
Vulcan Laser, 76
Wales, 91
walruses, 26, 27
water, 82, 88, 89
water cycle, 8
waves, 14
whales, 10, 26, 27
    watching of, 29
whale shark, 11
windsurfing, 15

X-Y
Xenia, Ohio, 44
X rays, 61, 71
Yellow River, 53
Yellowstone National Park, 5

Photo Credits

Our Watery Planet

Photodisc, Inc.—Page 7
Wayne & Karen Brown—Pages 10, 17, 22, 28
Michael J. Giudice—Pages 9, 29
François Gohier—Pages 17, 26, 27, 29
Tom & Pat Leeson—Page 27
NASA—Page 8
Norbert Wu—Pages 9, 21, 24, 25, 26, 30, 31
Al Giddings Images Inc.—Pages 23, 24
Vince Cavataio/Allsport USA—Page 14
AP/Wide World Photos—Pages 15, 22
AP/National Maritime Museum—Page 23
The Bettmann Archive—Page 12
Gamma Liaison—Page 13
Kaku Kurita/Gamma Liaison—Page 31
Pierre Perrin/Gamma Liaison—Page 29
Gamma Tokyo—Page 30
The Granger Collection—Pages 12, 13, 22, 26, 31
Doug Perrine: Innerspace Vision—Page 10
L. Dugast/Liaison International—Page 8
Kyle Leduc/Liaison International—Page 12
Carl Schneider/Liaison International—Page 15
Hamblin/Liaison International—Page 16
Paul Kennedy/Liaison International—Page 28
Paul Souders/Liaison International—Page 28
Nance Trueworthy/Liaison International—Page 16
Brandon Cole/Mo Young Productions—Page 16
Mark Conlin/ Mo Young Productions—Pages 21, 31
Darodents/Pacific Stock—Page 8
Reggie David/Pacific Stock—Pages 20, 21
Sharon Green/Pacific Stock—Page 9
William Bacon/ Photo Researchers—Page 27
Chesher/Photo Researchers—Page 23
David Hardy/Science Photo Library—Pages 15, 21
NASA/Science Photo Library—Page 14
Hal Beral/Visuals Unlimited—Page 11
David B. Fleetham/Visuals Unlimited—Page 20
Will Troyer/Visuals Unlimited—Page 11
Kevin Deacon/Waterhouse Stock Photography—Page 28
Stephen Frink/Waterhouse Stock Photography—Pages 18, 19
Marty Snyderman/Waterhouse Stock Photography—Pages 10, 25
James Watt/Waterhouse Stock Photography—Page 11

Illustrations: Howard S. Friedman—Pages 11, 14, 20, 21

In Nature's Path

Weatherstock—Page 33
AP/ WideWorld Photos—Pages 34-37, 40-55
Bettmann Archives—Pages 38, 39, 55
Superstock—Page 38
Kathleen Campbell/Liaison International—Page 39
Warren Faidley/International Stock—Page 34
Tom Carroll/International Stock—Page 40
Mike Howell/International Stock—Page 42
Horst Oesterwinter/International Stock—Page 43
Aaron Strong/Liaison International—Page 44
Gary Bigham/International Stock—Page 49
International Stock—Page 55
Patti McConville/The Image Bank—Page 48
Gamma Liaison/Figaro Magazine—Page 39
Porter Gifford/Gamma Liaison—Page 49
Steve Berman/Gamma Liaison—Page 49
Anthony Suau/Gamma Liaison—Page 54
National Center for Atmospheric Research/National Science Foundation—Pages 54-55

Illustrations: Wayne Hovis—Pages 34, 36, 45

Science Old and New

R. Barlow—Page 66
Scott Camazine/Photo Researchers—Page 57
Dr. E. R. Degginger—Page 69
Phil Degginger—Page 68
Marc Galindo/Custom Medical Stock—Page 56
Breck P. Kent—Pages 63, 68
Gerald L. Kooyman—Page 66
Carol Russo—Page 59
David Scharf—Pages 64-65
Dr. Kent A. Stevens/University of Oregon—Page 69
John Lundberg & John Sullivan—Page 66
AP/Wide World Photos/Jean Clottes—Page 70
AP/Wide World Photos/Michael Stephens—Page 63
AP/Wide World Photos—Page 73
UPI/Corbis-Bettmann—Page 63
EpConcepts/Custom Medical Stock—Page 60
NIH/Custom Medical Stock—Page 61
Larry Ulrich/DRK—Page 61
Shahn Kermani/Gamma Liaison—Page 60
Xavier Rossi/Gamma Liaison—Page 77
Gorilla Foundation—Page 67
The Granger Collection—Pages 58, 71
Michael Agliolo/International Stock—Pages 62-63
Muybridge/Mary Evans Picture Library—Page 59
Museum of Science, Boston—Page 76
B. Balick (University of Washington) & NASA—Page 72
D. Figer (UCLA) & NASA—Page 73
International Stock/NASA—Page 73
Bates Littlehales/National Geographic Society—Page 67
Joel Sartore/National Geographic Society—Page 67
National Photo Service—Page 71
George Steinmetz/National Geographic Society—Page 77
National Photo Service—Page 71
The Natural History Museum/Orbis—Page 69
Scott Camazine/Photo Researchers—Pages 78
John Foster/Photo Researchers—Pages 74-75
Tom McHugh/Photo Researchers—Page 70
Will & Deni McIntyre/Photo Researchers—Page 61
David Phillips/Photo Researchers—Pages 58-59
Michael Covington/Phototake NYC—Page 58
Roslin Institute/Phototake NYC—Page 62
Peter A. Simon/Phototake NYC—Page 79
Jean Claude Revy/Phototake NYC—Page 63
NASA/Phototake NYC—Page 74
Dr. Tony Brain/Science Photo Library—Page 65
Chris Butler/Science Photo Library—Page 72
Professors P.M. Motta & S. Correr/Science Photo Library—Page 64
A. B. Dowsett/Science Photo Library—Page 65
David Hardy/Science Photo Library—Pages 72-73
James Holmes/Cellmark Diagnostics/Science Photo Library—Page 62
James King-Holmes/Science Photo Library—Page 77
K.H. Kjeldsen/Science Photo Library—Page 65
Mehau Kulyk/Science Photo Library—Page 68
Matt Meadows/Science Photo Library—Page 78
Astrid & Hanns Frieder Michler/Science Photo Library—Page 60
Microfield Scientific LTD/Science Photo Library—Page 60
National Library of Medicine/Science Photo Library—Page 61
David Parker/Science Photo Library—Pages 64, 79
John Reader/Science Photo Library—Page 71
Sandia National Laboratories/Science Photo Library—Page 77
Science Photo Library—Page 75
Dr. Steve Gull; Dr. John Fielden; Dr. Alan Smith/Science Photo Library—Page 75

Dr. Linda Stannard, UCT/Science Photo Library—Page 65
Geoff Tompkinson/Science Photo Library—Page 79
Doe/Science Source—Page 59
Kraft/Explorer/Science Source—Page 75
LLNL/Science Source—Page 78
Alexander Tsiars/Science Source—Page 76
David M. Phillips/Visuals Unlimited—Page 64
Science VU/Visuals Unlimited—Page 71

Illustration: Jan Sovak—Pages 68, 69

Earth's Treasures

Breck P. Kent—Pages 82, 84-85, 87-90, 92-93, 95, 98, 101-102, 104
Wendell E. Wilson—Pages 80, 82, 92-93, 95-100
William E. Ferguson—Pages 83, 90-91, 93, 103-104
E. R. Degginger—Pages 85, 88, 91, 95, 97-99, 102
Phil Degginger—Page 81
Tino Hammid—Pages 96, 100-101, 103, 105
Jeff Scovil—Pages 97, 102-103
Michael Giudice—Pages 87, 90, 104-105
Wayne and Karen Brown—Page 104
Dominick Baccollo—Page 87
J. G. Edmanson/International Stock—Page 84
Oliver Massart/International Stock—Page 86
Roberto Arakaki/International Stock—Page 87
Stirling/International Stock—Page 91
Warren Faidley/International Stock—Page 94
Frank Grant/International Stock—Page 94
Floyd Holdman/International Stock—Page 99
John Michael/International Stock—Page 101
Gamma Liaison—Pages 93, 100
Bartholomew/Gamma Liaison—Page 105
Werner Krutein/Gamma Liaison—Page 83
Hoa-Qui/Gamma Liaison—Page 84
G.Brad Lewis/Gamma Liaison—Pages 87, 90
Richard Shock/Gamma Liaison—Page 89
Philippe Hurlin/Gamma Liaison—Page 91
Steve Morgan/Gamma Liaison—Page 95
Bob Schatz/Gamma Liaison—Page 97
Shahn Kermani/Gamma Liaison—Page 99
AP/Wide World Photos—Pages 83, 86, 93, 95

Illustrations: Howard S. Friedman—Pages 82, 99, 103

Cover: AP/Wide World Photos
Front end pages: Wayne & Karen Brown
Back end pages: AP/Wide World Photos

Scientific Consultants

Our Watery Planet
Steven L. Bailey
Curator of Fishes
New England Aquarium
Boston, Massachusetts

Science Old and New
Malcolm Fenton, PhD
The Dalton School
New York, New York

Earth's Treasures
Joseph Peters
American Museum of Natural History
New York, New York